CLASSIC
MOTORBIKES

Previous page: *1948 Indian*
Right: *Bimota Dieci*

C L A S S I C
MOTORBIKES

ROGER W. HICKS

Colour Library Books

CLB 2903
© 1992 Colour Library Books Ltd, Godalming, Surrey
This second edition published 1993
Printed and bound in Cordoba, Spain by Graficromo, S.A.
All rights reserved
ISBN 0 86283 965 3

Designed by **Nigel Duffield**

Edited by **Don Morley** and **David Gibbon**

Commissioning Editor **Andrew Preston**

CONTENTS

INTRODUCTION

Below: *When A.J.S. said "race-bred," they weren't kidding; the AJS 7R is only the best known of a long line of spectacular machines. By 1961, though, the glory was fading; there had been no special racers since 1954, and AMC twins like this were winning few significant races.*

Above: *Fully enclosed final drive was one of the many details which gave Sunbeams a reputation for reliability even in the 1920s.*

Right: *Postwar Velocettes were either classic, vintage-style singles like this or improbable-looking LE series twins (page 53).*

INTRODUCTION

Built in the light of Experience

THE UNAPPROACHABLE Norton THE WORLD'S BEST ROAD HOLDER

1954

CLOSE YOUR EYES and think of a classic motorcycle. Think of the smell of oil and hot metal. Think of a cacophony, a symphony of sounds, from the chuff... chuff...chuff of a pre-World War One single to the scream of a racer, via the rising and falling buzz-saw cadence of an off-road scrambler. Think of the tactile gloss of a Hesketh's tank under your fingertips; of the barked knuckles and the deleted expletive as you concede that, well, maybe it *does* need to cool down before you work on it. Think of the Futurist elegance of a Guzzi flat single, the industrial mass of a Harley Davidson, like a shipyard on wheels. Think of the understated arrogance of a BMW R100RS; of the Honda 90, like a puppy that follows you home.

Think of classic rides, too; of the gentle breeze in your face on a back-roads ride, of the wind clawing at you as the needle wavers past 140 mph on the *autobahn*. All of this is a part of appreciating classic motorcycles.

Not all motorcycles are classics. I know that mentioning the Honda 90 a couple of paragraphs back will surprise an awful lot of people. But no-one took the BSA Bantam seriously until they stopped making it, either, and the Velocette LE must be another

Above: *The engines on Norton's roadgoing twins were a far cry from the "cammy" singles on which their fame was built, but "The World's Best Road Holder" was no idle boast.*

Below: *A modern motorcycle like this Yamaha FZR400 delivers power that old-time racers could only dream of. Modern metallurgy and small, multi-cylinder engines allow very high engine speeds.*

INTRODUCTION

candidate for any informed motorcyclist's hall of fame. If you want some distinctly *un*-classic motorcycles, the last of the New Imps were pretty gruesome, and Harley-Davidson's Aermacchi-built Italian singles were for the most part ugly little things with cast-iron seats and electrics that would have made Joe Lucas blanch. Phelon and Moore's monstrously long-stroke Panther singles, affectionately dubbed "Big Pussies," were really only suitable for hauling huge sidecars very, very slowly, but there is a certain charm to the bang … bang … bang as the engine fires as it passes every second lamp-post.

Quite honestly, though, there has hardly ever been a motorcycle that was so bad, so utterly devoid of good points, that distance cannot lend it enchantment. I remember my brother's Moto-Guzzi Lodola as an incredibly sweet-handling motorcycle, conveniently forgetting that it was almost impossible to start (elderly Italian electrics again) and that where the gleaming red paintwork was concerned, it was a race between the oxidation that reduced the gleam to that of an egg-shell, and the inclination to fading in the sun that left one half of the tank red and the other half pink. For that matter, a friend of mine has recently bought a Suzi GT380, the original "rubber-frame special," and reckons it a classic; while the 500cc Kawasaki triples, one-dimensional motorcycles with slingshot acceleration and pig-on-stilts handling, are now rising somewhat in value.

In this book, I have tried to mix an appreciation of the universally acknowledged classics – the Broughs, the Sunbeams, the Indian twins and fours, the Vincents, the Manx Nortons, the Goldies – with some of the less stratospherically-priced motorcycles which still deserve "classic" status. I am absolutely sure that no-one in the world would make *exactly* the same selection, or give *quite* the same ratings as I have given to the different motorcycles in this book, but equally, I am sure that there are very few of us who would not (if we could afford it) give garage space to as many of them as we could collect.

Above: *Those very details which make a machine like this Brough Superior SS100 so handsome are the reason why it would be impossibly expensive to make such a machine today: innumerable finely-finished, hand-made parts assembled into a glorious whole.*

Left: *On a Honda Goldwing, like this 1984 Aspencade 1100 Special Edition, there is much that glitters; yet there is also some very impressive engineering in the powerful flat four, a layout which would have invited cooling problems in the days of iron engines and air cooling.*

Right: *For many, many years, Harley-Davidsons like this "shovelhead" have been more about style and looks than about the cutting edge of motorcycle technology. Even with a huge 80 cid (1340cc) engine, power from the narrow-angle, in-line V-twin is severely limited by the long stroke, the enormous reciprocating masses, and inefficient air-cooling.*

1

INVENTION
and
INNOVATION

Above: *A V-twin Harley classic
from 1915.* Main picture: *a 1913
Matchless T.T. racer.*

INVENTION and INNOVATION

THERE ARE MANY ways to appreciate a classic motorcycle. It can be a purely aesthetic experience, an elegant mechanical harmony. It can be purely technical, a fascination with the way in which brilliant (and not-so-brilliant) engineers solved engineering problems. It can be exclusivity, the pleasure of owning something that other people do not. It can be historical, either because of a particular innovation (the first machine with a positive-stop foot gear change, the first machine with six cylinders) or because of the achievements of the *marque* or of a particular motorcycle, such as Indian's 1-2-3 at the 1911 Isle of Man T.T.

Or, of course, it can be the pleasure of riding them. But quite honestly, for the first two or three decades that motorcycles existed, that pleasure was not unmitigated.

To begin with, there was no clutch. You started the 'bike the same way you started an Ordinary (penny-farthing) bicycle, by running alongside then jumping into the saddle when it was going; the approved term was "vaulting" into the saddle.

Think about this for a moment. There can be few motorcyclists who have not, at one time or another, had to "bump start" a motorcycle. The way you do it, though, is to put the 'bike in first or second, pull in the clutch, run alongside (or if you are lucky, roll downhill); and then, when you judge the rear wheel is turning fast enough to start the engine, you drop the clutch.

Ah, yes. The clutch. But these early machines had no clutch ....

Admittedly, compression ratios were very low indeed: typically three to one, with an "automatic" inlet valve (held closed only by a weak spring) and a mechanically-operated exhaust valve. The resistance that the cylinder offered was not great; but it still cannot have been much fun, and besides, once you were in motion you had to *stay* in motion. If you did not, the machine stalled.

If you have ever had the unfortunate experience of trying to navigate a motorcycle with a broken clutch cable, you might think you have some idea of the problems the early riders faced. Clutchless gear-changes are something you can master, and if you plan far enough ahead, it is amazing how you can wobble along in first gear at almost zero miles an hour, praying that the traffic light ahead will change. Of course, our motorcycling great-grandfathers did not have traffic lights to worry about, but they did not have gears either.

Actually, the very earliest motorcycles did not have this problem, because a steam engine develops maximum torque at zero rpm, and therefore requires neither a clutch nor a gearbox. As early as 1869, a Perreaux steam engine had been attached to a Michaux velocipede (a "boneshaker" of eighteenth-century ancestry), and the machine survives, in the Robert Grandseigne collection in France. An American, S.H. Roper, achieved something very similar within a year or two.

Another American, L.D. Copeland, went one better in 1885: he attached a steam engine to an "Ordinary" bicycle, though the small (steered) wheel was at the front and the big (driven) wheel was at the back. The steam motorcycle was, however, an intriguing dead-end; the way to the future was shown when Wilhelm Maybach rode Gottlieb Daimler's motorcycle (complete with outrigger "training wheels") on 10th November 1875, though this was not a production machine.

The first production, internal-combustion engine motorcycle was the Hildebrand and Wolfmüller of 1894: a 744cc twin with (extremely) direct drive to the rear hub. The connecting rods were actually connected to a crank on the rear wheel, and this terrifying machine was capable of 40 kph, almost 25 mph.

The next significant production motorcycle (as distinct from tricycles, of which there were several), was the Werner of 1897. This was the machine which popularized the phrase, "the dreaded side-slip." The 217cc single-cylinder engine was mounted on top of the front wheel, which it drove with a twisted rawhide belt. On slippery roads, the high centre of gravity frequently led to "the dreaded side-slip," and when the machine fell over, it could almost

Below: *J.A. Prestwich of Tottenham (London) built complete motorcycles from 1904 to 1908, after which they concentrated on supplying "loose" engines to other manufacturers. This pre-1914 example is a technically advanced pushrod ohv model.*

Above: *The original 1885 Daimler "Reitwagen," the grandfather of all motorcycles, was destroyed in a fire and today only replicas exist. Some can even be ridden, like the example photographed at Daytona in 1984 (facing page).*

be relied upon to burn. The petrol would spill from the tank, where it would promptly be ignited by the burner for the hot-tube ignition; and petrol in those days was much more volatile than it is today. A switch to electric ignition in about 1898 stopped the fires, but left the side-slip.

In 1901, though, the New Werner came along. Now the engine was fitted inside the frame of the bicycle, in place of the pedal bracket: the modern motorcycle had arrived. A matter of months later, Phelon and Moore had established their trade-mark (and the look of the modern motorcycle) by building the engine into the frame, with the cylinder stretching between the pedal bracket and the steering head.

There was still no clutch (a "free engine" in the jargon of the day), nor were there gears, and lubrication was still by "total loss," whereby the rider gave a squirt with a hand-pump when he remembered, and in due course the oil worked its way past the piston rings and burned, or dripped away, or mixed with road dust to create a wonderfully abrasive paste. Never mind; Messrs. P. & M. *did* add an expanding-clutch two-speed gearbox in 1905, a year after the first Triumph had appeared. Also, automatic inlet valves

1906 N.S.U. 3hp

NECKARSULM IN GERMANY LENT its name to the motorcycles built there, though the cumbersome name was soon shortened to NSU. This is not one of the very earliest models, which had Swiss-built Zedel 1.5 hp engines, but has the inlet-over-exhaust valve arrangement which characterized NSU's own power plants. There is no suspension except for the sprung saddle, unless you count the flexing of the frame and of the reinforced bicycle-style front forks, and the belt drive is direct: there is neither a gearbox nor a "free engine" (clutch). The lever on the drive side of the tank is the advance-retard control for the spark ignition. Braking is of course negligible.

"L.P.A." for "Light Pedal Assistance" was a euphemism with which our motorcycling forebears were all too familiar. Even without belt slip, hills often required manpower as well as mechanical horsepower.

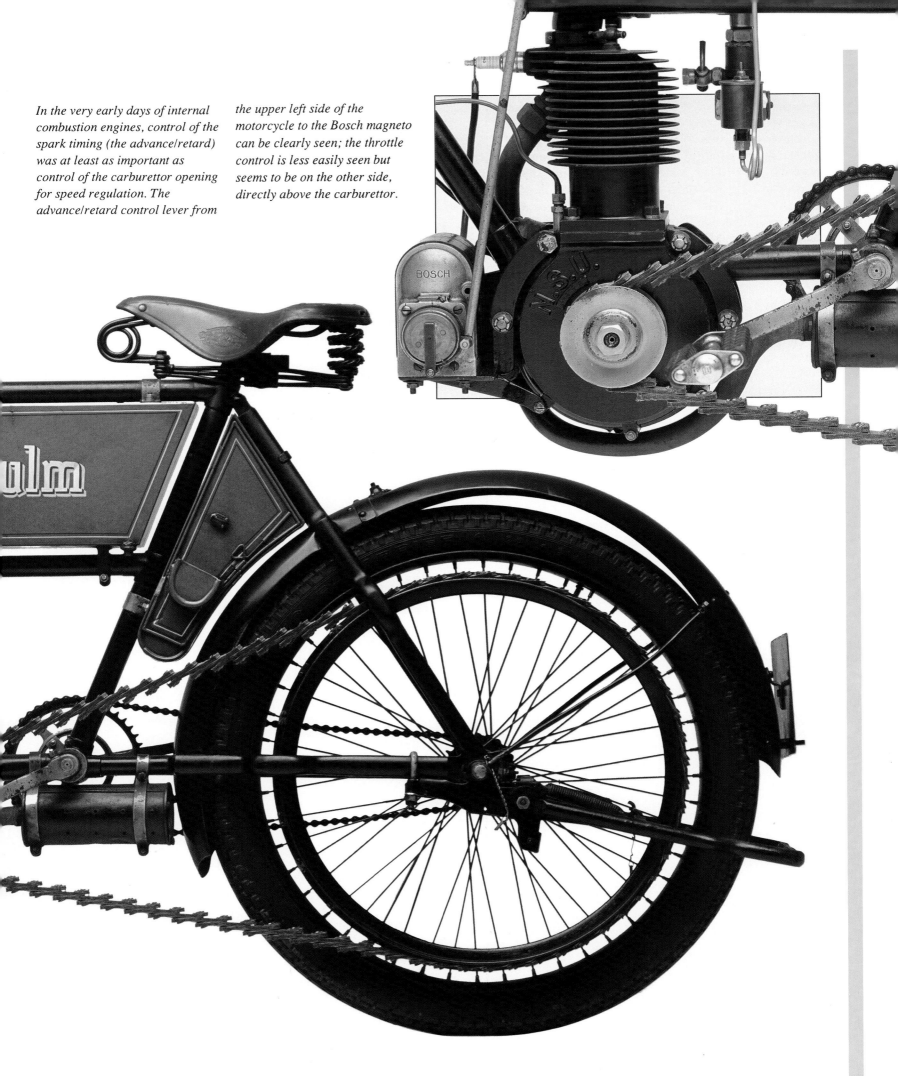

In the very early days of internal combustion engines, control of the spark timing (the advance/retard) was at least as important as control of the carburettor opening for speed regulation. The advance/retard control lever from the upper left side of the motorcycle to the Bosch magneto can be clearly seen; the throttle control is less easily seen but seems to be on the other side, directly above the carburettor.

Spark ignition was a marked improvement over the old "hot tube," which almost invariably started a fire if the machine fell over and fuel was spilled, though the old mica-insulated plugs were much less reliable (and much shorter-lived) than modern porcelain plugs. Another great step in the early years was the adoption of mechanically operated exhaust and inlet valves, instead of the "automatic" valve which was held closed by a weak spring and sucked in air as the piston fell on the induction stroke. The relatively modest finning on the engine was adequate to dispel the heat from a slow-revving, low-powered engine. The coils in the fuel-feed line to the carburettor are to reduce the risk of fracture due to vibration. All belt drives required frequent dressing and tightening, and even then they slipped badly in wet weather.

were on the way out, compression ratios were rising, and both valves were now likely to be mechanically operated.

Many well-known companies were in business by 1905, some still extant, some long gone. Royal Enfield was founded in 1898 to make motor-tricycles; Matchless followed in 1899; Norton was founded in 1898; and other British contemporaries included Rex, Raleigh, Singer, New Hudson and James. In the United States, Indian was founded in 1901, and Harley-Davidson in 1903, and in Switzerland both Motosacoche/MAG and Condor started making motorcycles at around this time.

There was still a great deal of experiment. J.A.P. made monster V-twins of 2700cc, while the French Buchet vertical-twin was reputed to displace 4525cc. A twin had many advantages over a single, of course. The power strokes came around more often, which meant that the ride was smoother (especially important on a single-gear, clutchless machine) and that you could afford to reduce the mass of the flywheel. The reciprocating and rotating masses were lower, which made for a more efficient, faster-revving engine (though 2000 rpm was still regarded as pretty fast); and if one cylinder failed, the other would probably get you home! Also, the V-twin engine fitted naturally into the motorcycle frame. The leader in motorcycle V-twins was J.A. Prestwich (J.A.P.), and by the time that Harley-Davidson got around to V-twins in 1909 they had already been adopted by a number of other companies. There were also in-line fours (Binks, 1903), flat twins (Fée, 1905), in-line and radial triples, V-fours, and water cooling (for the heads, not the cylinders), which appeared on the Scott in 1908.

The Scott was of course a two-stroke, and a two-stroke twin, at that; the hottest racing configuration of the early 1990s. The advantage of a two-stroke is that there is no "idle" cycle: the cylinder fires on every revolution. The increase in volumetric efficiency, the power obtained from a given swept volume, is therefore considerable; but the decrease in thermal efficiency, the power obtained from burning a given weight of fuel, is equally significant. The Scott was for many, many years the antithesis of the typical two-stroke, which was so small and low powered that

its relative inefficiency hardly mattered, and in any case, small, low-powered two-strokes are always more fuel-efficient than big, powerful ones.

In the years from about 1905 to 1914, the "free engine" (clutch) became more and more usual, and different types of gears started to come in: not just two-speed, but three-speed, four-speed, and even continuously variable models such as the Zenith Gradua and Rudge Multi, where pulling a lever or turning a "coffee-grinder" handle either changed the diameter of the engine pulley and moved the rear wheel (Zenith), or changed the diameter of both the engine pulley and the rear wheel pulley simultaneously (Rudge). Less fastidious engineers just changed the pulley size without adjusting the tension of the drive belt, which made for even shorter belt life than the Zenith and Rudge systems, as well as encouraging even more stretch and slip than belt drives normally manifested. Many

Above: *The rear wheel belongs to the Scott below, the earliest known survivor of this famous two-stroke marque. It is* extraordinary how A.A. Scott *managed to add so many complications to the essentially simple two-stroke.*

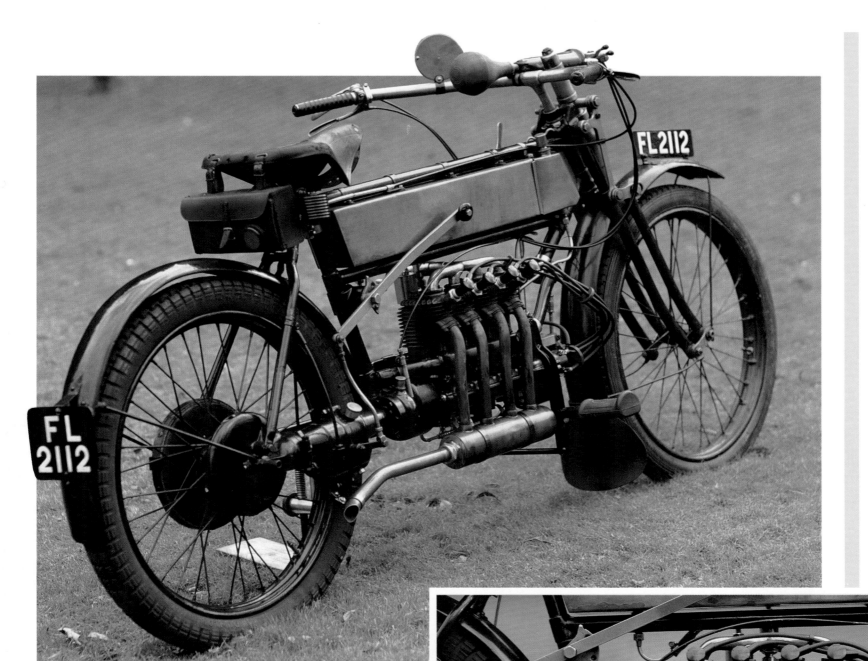

Above and right: *The Belgian FN company started making motorcycles in 1901 and were early believers in the four-cylinder layout. From 1904 to 1923 (this is a 1911 model) they always used shaft drive, which the smooth four-cylinder engine was well able to exploit, especially when equipped with a "free engine" and gearbox. To modern eyes, the four separate air-cooled cylinders with their exiguous finning may look strange, but this was a slow-revving engine built for torque and endurance rather than for sustained high-speed running.*

Left: *A.A. Scott was always keen on racing, and his motorcycles were very fast indeed – when they ran, which was by no means invariably. He was also a keen experimenter, building twins (like this) and triples. Some were air cooled, some were water cooled, and some were hybrids with water-cooled heads and air-cooled bores or vice versa.*

people felt, though, that the belt drive was still superior to the chain, precisely because it was not so harsh in the way it transmitted the power!

The belt was also cheaper to make, and it had another advantage that is not immediately obvious: if a hand-operated belt tensioner was fitted (as it often was), it could do double duty as a clutch if the tension was slacked off far enough. This accounts for the presence of what looks like a gear-lever on so many single-speed machines.

In general, most motorcycles were singles or V-twins, though there were a few fours, like the beautiful little 363cc F.N., made by the Belgian national munitions factory. This 1905 jewel was wonderfully smooth, and final drive was by a lovely miniature Kardan shaft the size of a knitting needle, with bevel drive at the rear axle. Not until 1908 did the machine grow a clutch or a gearbox, though, and even then it was only a two-speed affair.

1915 Harley-Davidson 11hp

IN 1915, HARLEY-DAVIDSONS already had half a dozen years' experience of building big, powerful V-twins. The 60.34 cid (989cc) engine dated from 1912 and powered a motorcycle that could hold its own anywhere in the world, on rutted tracks or on fast roads. The combined hand and foot clutch offered the rider reasonably easy control on hill starts (always a problem with foot-only clutches!) and the three-speed transmission operated by a left-hand lever was new in 1915, while all-chain drive was obviously the wave of the future.

The substantial gearbox with its complicated linkages is certainly boxy; but with three gears and a big, reliable, powerful engine the bicycle-style pedals were really only necessary for starting. This was just as well, because enthusiastic pedaling could all too easily bring the rider's toes into contact with the footboards. The rear brake pedal was just as massive and tractor-like as on modern Harleys.

Consider a hill start with this motorcycle. You are in neutral, with your right foot on the brake, balancing the machine with your left leg. You now pull the clutch with your left hand, and reach over with your right hand to engage "low" gear. Next, release the clutch with your left hand, and pull away smoothly. Now try to imagine the same procedure using only a foot clutch, with no handlebar-mounted brake ….

Although this motorcycle is not so equipped, you could, however, specify electric lighting on 1915 Harley-Davidsons! Another option not fitted here is a speedometer, which in those days was usually an after-market accessory.

As this rider's-eye view shows, the only handlebar controls are twist-grips: one for advance-retard, and the other for the throttle. There is no front brake, so that isn't a problem, but you do have to take your hands off the bars to operate the gear-shift and to operate the total-loss oil pump from time to time. In the event of a crash stop, all those protrusions on the tank could prove quite painful.

Various models of the F.N. four stayed in production until 1926, with varying sizes up to 748cc. In Britain, there was the wildly-improbable Wilkinson-TAC, with its bucket seat and steering wheel (later models had a handlebar). While any of these machines would qualify as a "classic," they were all pretty rare.

The real place for fours – big fours – was the United States. From their inception in 1911, Hendersons were in-line ioe (inlet-over-exhaust) fours (an advanced design for the time) mounted longitudinally in the frame. They were made in 1086cc, 1168cc and 1301cc, and at least some were equipped with a reverse gear, as well as a three-speed gearbox. In 1917 Bill Henderson sold his design to Schwinn (the bicycle makers), but evidently hankered to get back into the field: his Ace appeared in 1919, and therefore belongs in the next chapter. The 650cc Pierce Arrow was another American four which appeared in about 1909 and lasted only for four or five years. Once again, *all* American fours are classics.

Regardless of engine type or size, brakes remained casual in the extreme. Often, they were little more powerful than the bicycle brakes from which they derived, but traffic was not the problem in those days that it has since become. In fact, to this day you can badly frighten yourself by riding even a 1950s or 1960s motorcycle with drum brakes that are less than perfectly adjusted; we have become spoiled by disks!

In other words, it was not for quite a while that the motor cycle was anything that you would even want to attempt to drive on

Above: *This 2.75 hp Douglas from 1914 was typical of the "Douggies" that did sterling service as despatch bikes during World War I. Note, above right, the huge external flywheel.*

Above right: *Flat twins give a low centre of gravity and good handling, but to anyone used to bicycles they make the machine unacceptably wide (and impede pedaling) if mounted transversely. In 1914, cooling was not a major problem, so in-line mounting seemed like a good idea, though the front plug sometimes shorted in wet weather.*

Right: *You can clearly see the bicycle ancestry of this very smart 1915 Indian 680cc V-twin; but only four years before, machines cruder than this had been first, second and third on the Island.*

modern roads. Imagine even trying to start a motorcycle and sidecar without a "free engine."

For all of these reasons, the first "classic motorcycle" that I would actually want to ride would be something like a 1911 T.T. model Indian V-twin, with plenty of soft, woofly power, a plate clutch, a two-speed gearbox (albeit hand-change) and all-chain drive: primary chain to the gearbox, final chain to the rear wheel. And 1911 is a quarter of a century after Herr Benz's ingenious invention was first ridden on the road.

Then came the Great War, which proved a great spur to technical innovation: not immediately, but paradoxically by raising expectations and simultaneously denying them.

If you had been a British dispatch rider in the Great War, the first war in which motorcycles were widely used, you would probably have been issued with a 3.5 hp Sunbeam, a 4.25 hp BSA, a 4 hp Model H Triumph, or a 2.75 hp Douglas; or, in the Royal Flying Corps, maybe with a 3.5 hp P & M. Some had all-chain drive, some chain-cum-belt, but all had gearboxes, clutches and kick-starters.

Most of these machines would look reasonably familiar to a modern motorcyclist, apart from the old "flat tank" petrol tanks (the modern "saddle tank" did not become widespread until the 1920s) and the hand gear changes, but the fore-and-aft arrangement of the flat-twin "Douggie" would raise eyebrows to anyone brought up on BMW "boxers". The front plug was also distressingly subject to water-induced shorting in the mud of Flanders.

INVENTION and INNOVATION

For real fun, though, there there were various sidecar outfits. Some, such as the 3.5 hp P & M, or the seven-ninths hp Indian, were used for light passenger carrying, while the 3.75 hp Scott outfit and the five-sixths hp Clyno were fitted out as gunships, with a rear-facing machine-gun on the sidecar. This rearward configuration makes a lot of sense: after all, how often do you want to ride a motorcycle *towards* someone while firing large-calibre automatic weapons at them? Though it might have some appeal on the Los Angeles freeways.

The net result of the war was that reliability became first a Holy Grail, and then something that was taken for granted; and because the emphasis was on refining 1915 models and making them more reliable, rather than designing new models, there was an enormous pent-up demand on the side of the customers and a tremendous pent-up enthusiasm on the side of the designers when the end of the war came. Admittedly, the Americans were still designing motorcycles during the war, but with the rise of the cheap car they began to lose interest in two-wheeled vehicles; the motorcycle was already on its way to becoming what it is in America today, a toy rather than a means of utilitarian transport. The torch of leadership was passed from Indian to a whole host of European designers, most especially English designers.

These designers drew on aero engine experience, with its strides in metallurgy and engine "breathing"; on wartime experience,

Below: *With bicycle front brakes, and rear brakes that were not much more advanced, this 1913 MAG-engined Matchless was a T.T. racer. A Matchless had also won the very first T.T. in 1907.*

Right: *The first modern motorcycle: in 1901 (this is a 1903 2.75 hp) the Werner brothers established the basic layout of the motorcycle, especially the positioning of the engine.*

Above: *This 1914 Edmund, with its "adjustable spring frame," is the only known survivor of the 292 cc J.A.P.-engined model. Edmund, a small manufacturer, operated from 1907 to 1924.*

Right: *W.E. Brough, father of George of Brough Superior fame, made very fine in-line flat twins; this one dates from 1914. It is easy to see where young George got his feeling for quality.*

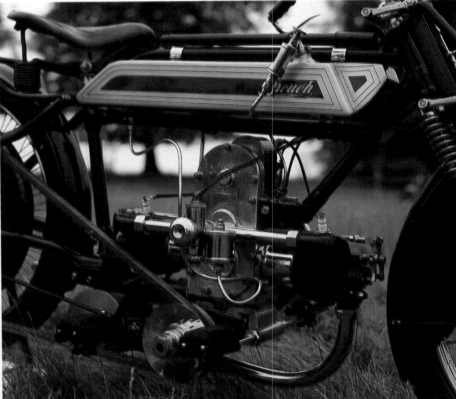

where a motorcycle was expected to carry its rider across almost anything; on the lessons of reliability that had perforce been learned; and upon a kind of frenzied creativity which was born in the realization that they had survived.

The last should not be underrated. The carnage of the "War to End Wars" was incredible. On the first day of the Somme offensive, the British took more casualties than the United States would take in the whole Vietnam war. In the words of J.R.R. Tolkien, who was a young man at the time of the war, "By 1918, all but one of my close friends were dead." The Roaring Twenties was at least in part a reaction to that. The old order was gone, and could never return. It would be a decade when every man wanted personal transport, and when a motorcycle was the only type of personal transport that most could afford; and it would be the decade when the first of the superbikes, the Brough Superior, would make its appearance. It would be the decade of everyman and superman.

2

*E*VERYMAN
—and—
*S*UPERMAN

Above: *Detail of the JAP single-cylinder 300 cc engine fitted to a 1926 Coventry Eagle.*
Main picture: *a 1926 Norton Model 19 Brooklands Racer.*

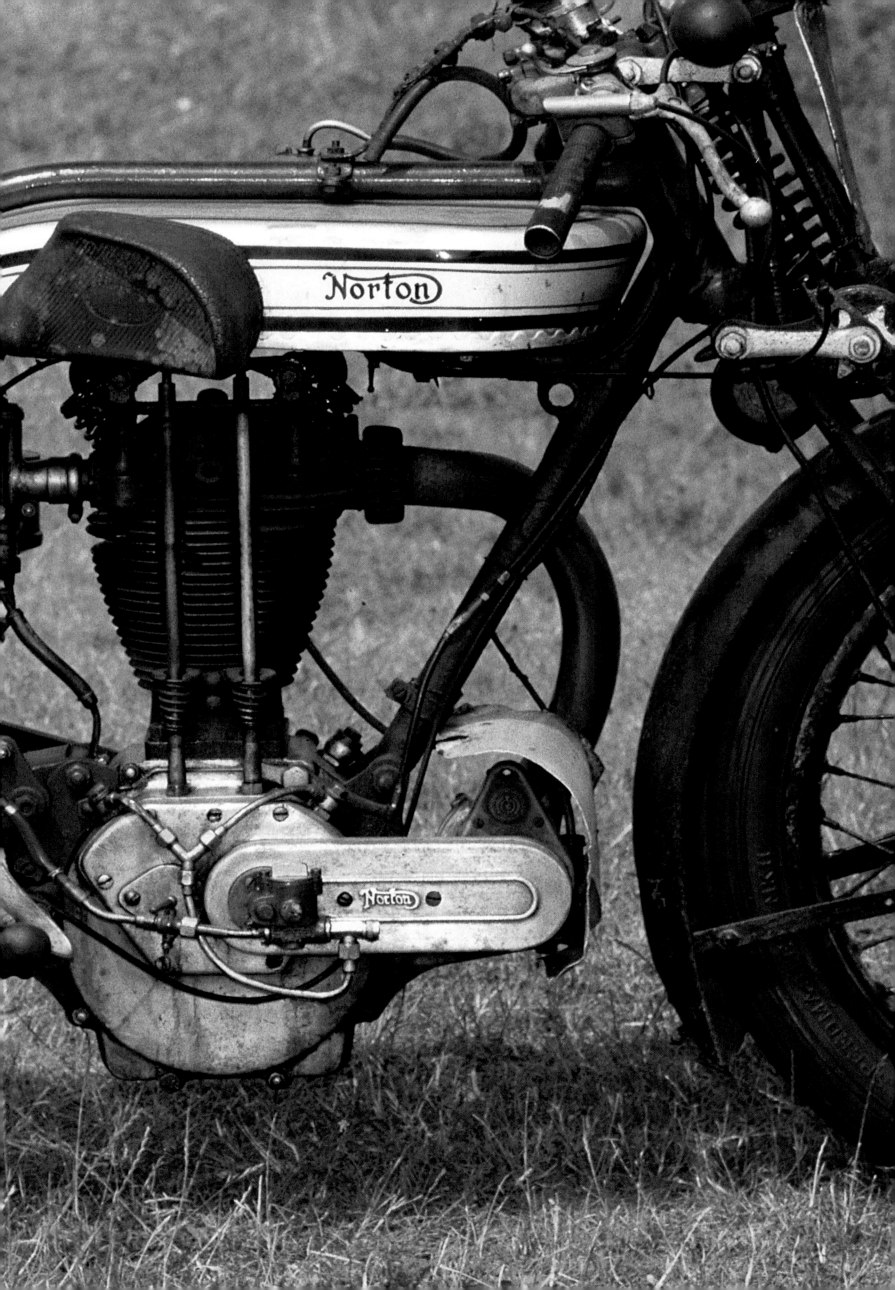

Everyman and Superman

A T THE 1919 Olympia Show in London, you could see (or at least get catalogues for) some two-hundred different models of motorcycle from more than a hundred different manufacturers. Most "manufacturers," of course, might better be called assemblers; they bought an engine here, a gearbox there, had a frame made somewhere else, subcontracted the petrol tanks to yet another company, and then completed the package with proprietary seats, controls, handlebars, wheels and so forth.

The materials they had to work with, though, were wonderful. Everyday or "cooking" engines still breathed asthmatically through tiny side valves, with very conservative timing, and had cheap pistons made of cast iron, but for anyone who wanted power, it was beginning to be offered in hitherto unimaginable quantities.

Breathing was one of the biggest differences. Overhead valves, and even overhead cams, offered far more efficient combustion spaces. The valves were bigger, so more mixture could be inhaled and exhaled, and there might even be four valves per cylinder. Valve overlap had been discovered, too: now, with improved understanding of gas flow within the cylinder, the inlet valve(s) might well start to open just before the exhaust valve had started to shut. All these improvements also meant that higher compression ratios could be used, which in turn translated into higher efficiency.

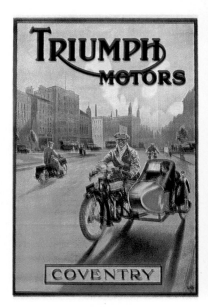

Right: *The motorcycle in the foreground is an overhead-valve Ricardo model of about 1923 with the four-valve head; "for there is no new thing under the sun." The side-car is a Gloria.*

Below: *A leading proponent of four-valve heads, and perhaps the best-known, was Rudge. This is their most famous model, the Ulster 500cc single dating from about 1929, but they made many other four-valves, including roadsters.*

Above and below: *This 500cc Norton CS1 won the 1927 T.T. The CS1 was the first production ohc Norton, introduced in 1928, and "cammy" Nortons would define single-cylinder Senior racing until singles could race no more against the rising tide of faster-revving multi-cylinder engines in the late 1950s, but their racing life was a good three decades.*

What was more, light-alloy pistons were much lighter than the old cast iron ones, and lower reciprocating masses meant less vibration, lighter engines, and the potential for much higher engine speeds: 4,000 rpm became entirely reasonable, and J.A.P. were looking at engines which ran at unprecedentedly high speeds, such as 6000 rpm.

Perhaps strangely to modern eyes, all these improvements were rarely applied to big engines. Instead, they were applied to 350cc and 500cc singles: these, of course, corresponding to the Junior and Senior categories of the Isle of Man Tourist Trophy. The foundations of the British tradition of light, fast, nimble singles were being established, but it is hard not to wonder what would have happened if the premier British race (and arguably the greatest motorcycle road race in the world) had been better supplied with long straights, and fewer hills and hairpin bends. The analogy with Indianapolis racing cars is irresistible: the totally-undemanding "brickyard" course has no hills and no hairpin bends, and the corners all go in the same direction. The result there has been cars that are blindingly fast, but bear absolutely no relation to the real world.

The Ricardo-designed Triumph single of 1921 had a pushrod-operated, four-valve head, though the valve gear was still out in the open air with no more lubrication than the rider might add from time to time with his oil can. On the other hand, a single overhead cam driven by a spur-and-bevel arrangement (and perforce enclosed) appeared as early as 1924 on the Velocette 350.

1924 Sunbeam (Model 3)

THIS SUNBEAM S3 WAS one of the last Marston machines, before the company was sold to I.C.I. in the late 1920s; then to Associated Motorcycles from 1937 to the eve of World War Two, when it was sold again to the B.S.A. group. While they might lack the fire of, say, a Rudge Ulster or a KTT Velocette, Sunbeams were not slow and they could confidently claim to be the best made and best finished of all British singles, which is to say, the best made and best finished of any singles, anywhere.

Both the primary and secondary drives ran in fully-enclosed chain cases, somewhat whimsically labelled "The Sunbeam Little Oil Bath Chain Case."

"Fir-cone" cooling caps over the inlet valve were de rigueur for side-valve engines with any pretences to performance, though the finning on the barrel and head suggests that no great quantities of heat needed to be dissipated elsewhere; while the diminutive carburettor on its long, thin inlet tract hardly argues for a racer. It all looks very vintage, though.

Note also the distinctly vintage priming cock for introducing neat petrol to the cylinder for starting; it has its own little feed and petcock from the black and gold tank. The huge, cast-alloy footrests are what give the clearest idea of the designer's priorities: reliable, long-distance touring comfort, rather than maximum all-out speed.

The extremely small frontal area of vintage motorcycles explains how they could go quite fast with relatively little power.

THE SUNBEAM

H 5074

As befitted a machine where everything was designed for the rider's convenience, there are two wheel stands, fore and aft; this was before centre-stands and side stands became the norm. The tank is liberally supplied with sight-glasses (lubrication was still total-loss, with a pump at the left front of the tank), but the Bonniksen speedometer is an accessory.

The gear-shift is on the right, unlike the Harley-Davidson on pages 18 and 19, and the clutch and brake levers are elegantly reversed; but the throttle is still the old-fashioned "lawn-mower" type of thumb lever, rather than a twist-grip, and the head and tail lights are still of the acetylene type: less for seeing than for being seen.

EVERYMAN and SUPERMAN

All through the 1920s and the 1930s, the single was refined and made faster-revving, more reliable, and more powerful. The best-known of the four-valve machines was probably the Rudge Ulster of 1929, a 500cc road/racing development of the design they had introduced in 1924, while the "cammy" or single overhead cam Nortons were the definitive overhead cam machines. The racing CS 1 dated from 1927, but the 1935 Norton International (the "Inter") was available as a genuine road-going motorcycle with lights, as was its contemporary, the KTT Velocette.

Around 1930, following Velocette's lead, all the sporting manufacturers began to abandon hand-changes for positive-stop, foot-change gears, and the "lawnmower" thumb-lever throttle gave way to the twist-grip pioneered by Indian. In other words, a single of the early 1930s was getting steadily closer to a modern motorcycle, without however giving up its essential simplicity and charm. The main thing that a modern rider might find less than charming was the rigid frame, though the still-feeble brakes might also provoke disquiet. Also, although they were much lighter than modern 'bikes, the machines of the 1920s and 1930s were also considerably less powerful; a point to which we shall return later in this chapter.

For the most part, the big V-twin was left as it was, side valves and all. It provided plenty of power for hauling a sidecar, and in those days sidecars were not just used as a way of carrying more people (or for carrying girlfriends, wives, and families in more comfort). They were also used in much the same way that light vans are used today: there were box delivery sidecars, open cargo-carrying sidecars, and specialist sidecars for tradesmen who made

Below: *The first overhead-cam Velocette appeared in 1925, with 350cc and performance to lick many a 500: the KSS (this one dates from 1930) was a classic British high-performance single, in the same sober black and gold livery as a Sunbeam, but much quicker.*

Above: *The Norton CS1 (1928) was the first overhead-cam Norton. Positive-stop foot shifts and high-performance spring frames might lie in the future, but "cammy" Norton engines would rule the roost for a quarter of a century or more.*

Right: *George Brough believed to a large extent in the old American saying, "You can't beat cubes." The SS80, introduced in 1924, may have had side valves; but with its J.A.P. 988cc engine, it was guaranteed in writing to have exceeded 80 mph (129 kph).*

"house calls," such as plumbers, chimney sweeps and so forth. As a small boy in the 1950s, the author can recall that an "outfit" was still the normal means of transport for window-cleaners, and even for the occasional chimney-sweep.

There were, however, always a few people who wanted *serious* power, the kind of power that was attainable only through a combination of large engines *and* the latest in high technology. J.A.P., Anzani, Harley-Davidson and Indian all experimented with four-valve heads for racing, and conservative two-valve, overhead-valve designs were offered for road use; but Anzani actually sold their rip-roaring, eight-valve V-twin to manufacturers of road-going motorcycles, notably the McEvoy-Anzani and the Krammer-Anzani. These were arguably the ultimate superbikes of the 1920s, though neither make (one British, the other Austrian) lasted for more than about half a decade, and neither sold more than a handful of machines with those engines.

The definitive superbike, though, was introduced in 1919: the Brough Superior. The name "Superior" came from the intention of its designer, George Brough, to build a motorcycle that was the ultimate in luxury and high performance. He was unable to persuade his father, William Brough, to introduce such a machine under the Brough name: Brough the elder had been making motorcycles since the first decade of the century, but was wedded to fore-and-

Everyman and Superman

aft flat twins, which he continued to make until 1923. On perfectly amicable terms, therefore, George set up on his own to make the Brough Superior.

The new Brough Superior was a knockout. It was amongst the first motorcycles to be fitted with a "saddle tank," the kind of petrol tank which we now take for granted, and everything about the machine was fitted and finished to the very highest degree of perfection. As with many lesser makers, just about everything was bought in, but this does not mean that the various components were "off-the-shelf." Rather, it means that the best components from the best makers were found, and then in many cases were finished still more carefully for the Brough. The analogy is not with buying (say) a stock Harley Davidson engine off the shelf; rather, it is with buying a racing engine and then having it blueprinted by the racing department.

The top-of-the-line machine boasted an side-valve J.A.P. 50-degree V-twin of 986cc (the "90 bore"), with light alloy pistons,

Right: *The Brough Superior SS100 first appeared in late 1924 (for the 1925 season) with an almost square 85.5 x 86mm engine of 980cc, a derivative of the old "90 bore" J.A.P. Finning was comprehensive; lubrication was by mechanical pump, albeit still total-loss with a claimed oil consumption of about 1450 mpg. This was the machine that was supplied with a certificate from the Brooklands track authorities certifying that it had completed a kilometre at 100 mph or more.*

Left and facing page bottom: *A cornfield may not seem like the natural habitat of a 1939 Brough Superior SS100, but the big V-twin (available with a choice of 996cc J.A.P. or 990cc AMC/Matchless engines) would have been expected by most of its owners to traverse such terrain without complaint, while still delivering up to 120 mph on the open road. Apart from the reversed levers and the (well concealed) rigid frame, this is a machine that would not have looked too much out of place a decade or two later.*

Below: *His friends called him "T.E." because the surname varied: Shaw, Ross, and Lawrence. Others called him "El Aurans" or Lawrence of Arabia. He called at least one of his Brough Superiors "Boanerges," a son of Thunder. This is one of a series of Brough Superior motorcycles that he owned; after the accident in which he was killed (on a Brough, avoiding some delivery boys), George Brough kept the last machine El Aurans had ordered and rode it himself.*

driving through a 3-speed Sturmey-Archer gearbox. As alternatives, you could get a 988cc J.A.P. side-valve or a 748cc ioe engine from M.A.G.; and then, shortly afterwards, there was the option of a 999cc Barr and Stroud sleeve-valve engine.

The bikes were a success, and George was encouraged; and so for the 1924 season he brought out the S.S. 80, with a 988cc J.A.P. engine and guaranteed *in writing* to have been tested at Brooklands at more than 80 mph (128 kph). A year later came the all-time legend, the S.S. 100. As with the S.S. 80, every machine was individually tested, and the SS 100 was guaranteed to have exceeded 100 mph (160 kph).

Even today, 100 mph is not slow; comparatively few people have ever ridden a motorcycle at such a speed. The first time you do it, the experience is unforgettable. Roads which had previously seemed to be fairly straight are suddenly revealed as remarkably twisty, and instead of planning a few tens of yards ahead, you find yourself planning hundreds of yards ahead. The strangest thing, though, is the way in which you get the illusion that you are standing still, and that the world is rushing past you like some sort of video game. Eventually, as you become used to riding at very high speeds, this sensation disappears, though it can come back if you make another significant increase in speed. After becoming accustomed to speeds of 100-110 mph (160-175 kph), for example, speeds over 130 mph (210 kph) still seem very high. Presumably one can break through this barrier too, but there are not many opportunities unless you take to the racetrack.

Right and below: *Not all Harley-Davidson twins were V-twins: the fore-and-aft 1920 "electric sport model" was a flat twin in the Douglas tradition. Despite the relatively diminutive engine and the "Sport" designation, it was essentially a heavy tourer with a fully enclosed chain and a wonderfully low centre of gravity which made it easy to handle on the appalling American roads of the period. It was never widely accepted by conservative customers, though, and the only other Harley flat twin was the transverse-engined, shaft-drive XA, of which a thousand were made for the U.S. army in World War Two.*

If riding at very high speeds is like this on today's thoroughfares, with wide, smooth roads and efficient triple disk brakes to drag you down from such velocities, what must it have been like for riders of the 1920s?

Not only were road surfaces poor, and roads narrow; the motorcycles of the day had very limited front suspension, and few had any rear suspension at all. The old, sprung "tractor saddles" were considerably more comfortable than might be thought, but they were still not a patch on rear suspension. Again, it is true that traffic did not amount to much; but as anyone who has ridden in, say, India can assure you, it does not *need* to amount to much. A single farm cart pulling out of a field, or even a dog asleep in the road when you round a corner, can make you wish for very powerful brakes indeed. Remember, too, that twist-grip throttles were by no means universal: Indian had introduced them in 1906, but even machines like the Brough often used "lawn-mower" thumb-lever throttles.

Nevertheless, we are coming a lot closer to a genuine, ridable classic with the Brough. If you have the good fortune to ride one nowadays, the first thing that you are likely to notice is how light the machine is: this is how Broughs and others managed to be so fast, despite their relatively low power outputs: the S.S. 80 delivered something like 25 bhp. Then you are surprised at the tractability of the engine; as no less a person than Lawrence of Arabia once said of his Brough "Boanerges," "Boa is a top-gear machine, as sweet

Above: *Champion plugs gave New York's Finest the edge over the speeding motorist, at least that is the suggestion in this 1930s advertisement. The patrolman's Harley Stream-Line, introduced in 1925 and featuring the now-familiar teardrop shaped tank, no doubt played its part. Both twins, as shown, and singles were included in the range. Front wheel brakes, absent on this model, were introduced some two years later.*

Right: *Indians are usually painted red – reasonably enough, perhaps – but this Indian Scout is particularly handsome. It was not, however, particularly powerful, and Indians were no longer on the cutting edge of motorcycle development. This one dates from about 1927, the year after the 37 cid (600cc) engine was upped to 45 cid (737 cc) and acquired detachable, Ricardo-type heads.*

in that as most single-cylinders in middle. I chug lordlily past the guard-room and through the speed limit at no more than sixteen."

The petrol tank, with its twin fillers tightened by tommy-bars, forces your knees rather further apart than you may be used to with a modern machine, but the engine is remarkably quiet, at least at the kind of speeds that you are likely to essay today. What is more, you could expect to get 80 miles to the (imperial) gallon of petrol, or to consume 3.6 litres per 100km; about the same as a 1990 Enfield India 500cc single

There were other Broughs too. The smallest, for the 1931 season, was 498cc (62.5mm x 80mm), but still a V-twin. Then there was the eggshell-black Black Alpine with its 680cc ohv J.A.P. engine housed in a Draper and Draper spring frame. Or the straight four with the Austin engine and the twin rear wheels laced to a single hub and intended primarily for sidecar use: several of these very rare machines survive, and are still ridden. Or many "show specials," such as the 1927 V4; the 1928 in-line four with its specially-made M.A.G. engine; or the double-flat-twin Golden Dream. And then World War Two came along. Brough went over to manufacturing war matériel; and after the war he apparently

decided that the in-house, 90-degree V-twin that was under development would be too expensive, so he just stopped making motorcycles.

If you had a weakness for large, powerful motorcycles but preferred your mounts to come from the other side of the Atlantic, you had a choice in the 1920s that spanned quite a range, with makes like Ace, Excelsior, Henderson, and more; but the main players were always Indian and Harley-Davidson.

During the Great War, Harley-Davidson's "Wrecking Crew" had toppled Indian from their competition pre-eminence. Both sides raced big twins, but both sides seemed content to reserve their technical fireworks for the track, and to sell rather pedestrian side-valve machines to the public. In 1921, though, Harley-Davidson introduced their first 74 cid (1213cc) twin, a step up from the old 61-inch (1000cc), with the added advantages of a detachable head with ioe valves. The nominal horsepower was 9.5, but the torque was titanic; in horse parlance these were Suffolk Punches, Percherons and Clydesdales, not Japanese-style ponies. In 1924 they switched from cast-iron to light-alloy pistons, and in 1926 they finally abandoned the "flat tank" design (by now very dated,

1926 Coventry Eagle 300cc

Front suspension was pretty much taken for granted, often with complex twin-pillar arrangements, but all that coddled the rump of the typical rider was a sprung saddle from Brooks or someone similar.

COVENTRY EAGLE IS NOT a name which springs unbidden to the lips today, but from 1901 to 1939 this former bicycle factory assembled some first-class motorcycles with a variety of engines. This 300cc J.A.P.-engined machine is not one of the "greats" (Bert Le Vack broke records in the 1920s with J.A.P. V-twins in Coventry-Eagle frames), but the handling was such that only the most careless or inexperienced rider was likely to find himself in unexpected trouble, and the styling was as modern as you could wish, with the new-fangled "saddle" tank popularized by Brough Superior.

Albion gearboxes were a popular alternative to Sturmey-Archer, and (like most) this is a three-speed unit: "Low," "Middle" and "High." The primary drive was still out in the open, but flexible sections of fuel and oil pipe were now replacing the elaborately-coiled solid metal tubing of old. Note the appearance of both "J.A.P." and "Coventry Eagle" on the engine.

Restoring the electrics of vintage machines is always a dilemma. No doubt the original manufacturers would have used a handsome, yellow-and-orange candy-striped high tension lead if it had been available, but concours judges would award higher points for black rubber (and a vintage plug). For a motorcycle that is to be ridden – which is after all the primary purpose of a motorcycle – then surely modern HT leads are the way to go. By the same token, any modern tyre will offer more grip, and be much safer, than the original stock item. The reversed controls are a charming period touch which should never be altered, however.

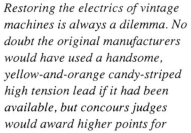

Headlamps were still very much an afterthought, as witness the somewhat laboured brackets, and as many preferred the simple and comprehensible acetylene variety as advocated the (slightly) brighter electrical type – which was much more convenient, as long as it worked. Reversed levers were, however, in their prime; they actually fit the hand better than the usual kind.

and not at all the thing for an up-market machine) and adopted a "teardrop" or saddle tank. Incredibly, though, that was about it: not until 1929 did they bother to do anything new to the engineering, despite the explosion of new designs in Europe.

In 1929 they brought out the new 45 cid (750cc) motorcycle with a side-valve engine, a 3-speed gearbox, foot clutch and hand change. At the time, this was old-fashioned but not absurdly so; by 1951, when it ceased production, it was a dinosaur. The flathead 45 was a "classic" in the same sense that a Honda 90 or an NSU Quickly is a "classic": a bulletproof machine that could resist immense abuse, though it lacked the technical sophistication (relative to 1929) that the overhead-cam Honda 90 had when it came out. The only bike that I would call a "classic" in the whole line-up was the deadly-slow, 3-wheeler Servi-Car, beloved of American traffic police and still in production (still with a side-valve motor and a hand gear change) in 1974; a living fossil.

Then, in 1930, they brought out the worst Harley of all time, the 74 cid VL. Anyone who calls that dog a "classic" is wearing spectacles that are not merely rose-tinted; they must be opaque. Just about everything used to break or fail, and the monstrosity stayed in production for a decade! The 1936 80 cid (1312cc) side-valve machine was infinitely more reliable, and just about commands "classic" status, but the first *real* classics in literally decades were

the overhead-valve 61 cid (1936) and 74 cid (1941) "knuckleheads," and they are really the antecedents of the next chapter.

If you didn't like Harleys, there were always Indians. Unfortunately, they too had regressed from their position of technical pre-eminence. When World War One was over, you could get 37 cid (606cc), 61 cid (1000cc) and 74 cid (1213cc) motors, but the smallest (the Scout) was arguably the best, with geared primary drive, a three-speed gearbox, and about 12 bhp. In 1925, the whole range acquired detachable heads, too.

In 1927, the Scout went to 45 cid. This was a nice bike, but someone discovered that you could turn down the flywheels of a Chief, shorten the pistons, and fit the whole show into the bottom end of the Scout to create the "Stroker Scout" with 57 cid (934cc), and a good chance of taking on a 74-inch machine and winning. Maybe the British did have the right idea with smaller, nimbler bikes, after all!

In the 1930s, Indian twins acquired dry-sump lubrication (previous models had been throttle-controlled, total-loss), a 4-speed shift, and even light-alloy barrels and high-compression heads (the Y-type motor, as distinct from the G-type) in 1935. Even so, technical innovation was slow, and the only way that Indians were really "classics" in the 1930s was in the same way that Harley-Davidsons and Indian Enfields are classics today: living

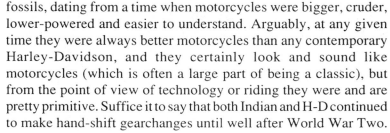

Above: *The Matchless Silver Hawk was a 593cc narrow-angle (18 degree) V4. It was produced only for a short time (it was introduced early in the Great Depression), but it shows that V4 motorcycles are nothing very new.*

Left: *The Danish-built Nimbus was never a likely motorcycle, but in its way it was very handsome. From 1920 to 1957 it retained the same basic layout, a light frame with an in-line, air-cooled 746cc engine of modest power and estimable smoothness and reliability.*

Below: *The 596 cc Ariel Square Four or "Squariel" was essentially two parallel twins with geared crankshafts. The original engine was smooth, but prone to overheating at the rear. This is the redesigned version (1936).*

fossils, dating from a time when motorcycles were bigger, cruder, lower-powered and easier to understand. Arguably, at any given time they were always better motorcycles than any contemporary Harley-Davidson, and they certainly look and sound like motorcycles (which is often a large part of being a classic), but from the point of view of technology or riding they were and are pretty primitive. Suffice it to say that both Indian and H-D continued to make hand-shift gearchanges until well after World War Two.

Of course, motorcycling in the United States is a very different experience from motorcycling in Europe, even today. Distances are very much greater, which places a premium on big, heavy machines; maintenance is casual, and the motorcycle has since the 1920s been less a means of transport than a toy, because of the availability of the cheap motor-car. The big twins were not the only way to get a big motorcycle: another was a big four.

As we saw in the last chapter, air-cooled, in-line, longitudinally-mounted fours were nothing new; and the fours for the 1920s were very much a continuation of previous design philosophies. The Henderson remained in production under the aegis of Schwinn until 1931, when the factory went over to producing only pedal cycles; but the once-classic machines were by now looking very old-fashioned (though supremely smooth).

Bill Henderson's Ace appeared in 1919 with an 1168cc engine, but later grew to 1229cc and 1266cc; for a four it was quite technically advanced, with light-alloy pistons and Henderson's favourite ioe valve actuation. Henderson was killed in 1922 when testing a new model, and although Arthur Lemon kept the Ace name alive, the company had financial problems and was taken over in 1927 by Indian, who called the machine first the Indian Ace and then (after 1931) just the Indian Four; it disappeared a few years later.

The Cleveland four entered production as a 746cc design in about 1925, and a 996cc version was made from 1928 to 1929, when the company shut up shop for good. As stated in the last chapter, *all* American fours are classics, but only Indians, Hendersons and the occasional Ace are likely to be encountered.

Another in-line four which deserves classic status is the Danish-built Nimbus. Introduced in 1920, it was a 750cc air-cooled, in-line four with exposed ioe valve gear and with the petrol contained in a large-diameter top tube. At 380 pounds it was remarkably light for a "four," largely as a result of the extensive use of pressed steel in the frame, but it was most assuredly *not* a sporting machine; the extra cylinders were for smoothness, torque, and reliability. The same basic design was steadily developed for many years, and production ceased only in 1957. By that time, the petrol tank looked a bit more conventional and the engine had grown an overhead cam, but it was still an air-cooled, longitudinally mounted in-line four; certainly the last of the breed in series production. The manufacturers, Fisker and Nielsen, are perhaps better known for

EVERYMAN and SUPERMAN

their Nilfisk vacuum cleaners, which also benefit from better advertising and a more aggressive export policy.

There were, however, several other options than singles, V-twins and in-line fours. At the outright demented end of the scale, there was the 640cc 5-cylinder radial engine built into the front wheel of the Megola. This German machine reputedly handled very well, because of the low centre of gravity and the front-wheel drive, but there were no gears and there was no clutch, an incredible omission in 1921, when the machine was introduced, and doubtless a contributing factor in its demise just four years later, by which time almost two thousand had been made. You could, however, change "gear" ratios by the simple expedient of changing the size of the front wheel …. In all fairness, you could get away with some pretty wild ideas in Germany, because in the aftermath of the Great War few could afford to run motor-cars, but many could afford motor cycles.

Back in England, Matchless's 593cc narrow-angle (26-degree) V4 "Silver Hawk" is probably a classic – it is certainly rare enough – but it had the misfortune to be born on the eve of the Depression, in 1929. Essentially two of the equally-unlikely Silver Arrow transverse V-twins in a common block, the overhead-cam engine looked beautiful, but it would almost certainly have suffered from overheated rear cylinders if it had been ridden hard.

Left: By 1929, when this 745cc R62 was made, BMW had been making flat twins for half-a-dozen years. Power had risen from 8.5 bhp for the 494cc R32 of 1923 to 24 bhp for the 734cc ohv R63 of 1928/9.

Below: BMW made many people (especially Norton) very unhappy when Georg Meier won the Senior T.T. in 1939 with this elegant, fully-sprung, lightweight, 70 bhp supercharged 500cc racer.

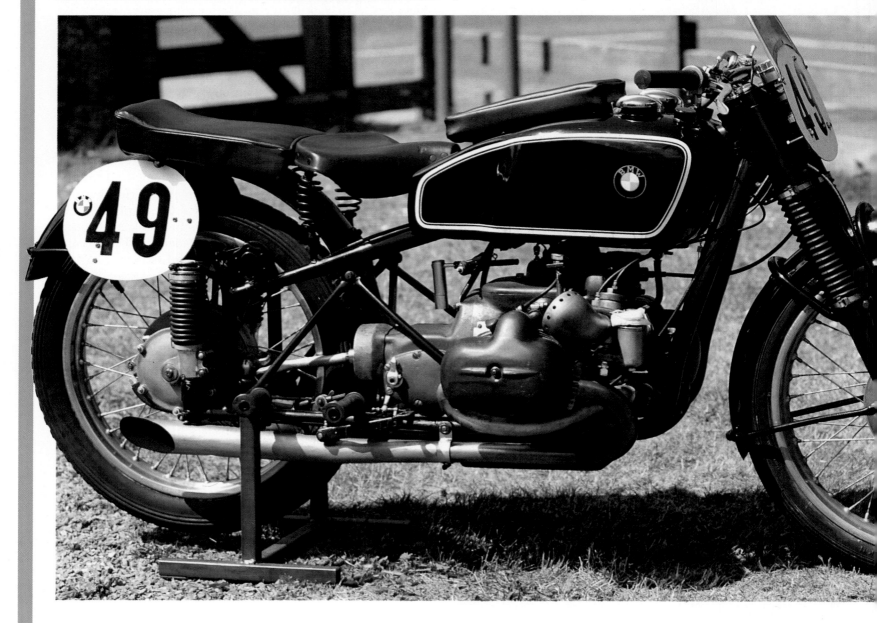

The Ariel Square Four, or "Squariel," certainly *did* suffer from overheating rear cylinders. This improbable design was introduced as a 498cc machine in 1931, and effectively consisted of two parallel twins geared together at the crankshafts. The four equidistantly-spaced bores really did form a square, and while the design was wonderfully smooth and powerful if you rode it as sedately as its makers intended, there were inevitably those who desired to use all of the power, all of the time. With air cooling, this just was not on, and you could warp the heads or seize the rear cylinders if you tried. Like the Matchless Silver Hawk, it was an overhead-cam design. With increased capacity (a nominal 1000cc, available after 1935) and a forest of push-rods instead of an overhead cam, it would survive for many years. Any Squariel is most assuredly a classic.

Reputedly, F.N. made a flat four in 1937 for the Belgian army, and of course George Brough's "Golden Dream" was a pair of flat twins geared together in much the same way as a Square Four; something that is not immediately obvious, however, is that the two twins were "stacked" one above the other, for the best possible cooling. Several Golden Dream prototypes were made; one is still in use and another is at the National Motorcycle Museum in Birmingham, England.

Vastly more practical than any of these was the transverse flat twin. Granville Bradshaw's ABC of 1919 showed the way. It was definitely a classic, but not one that you would have much hope of riding very far: unreliable valve gear and poor lubrication did the company in, largely as a result of guarantee claims. Even so, the overhead valve 398cc machine with its 4-speed gearbox, all in a spring frame, was well ahead of its time. Although ABC went into liquidation in 1921 (along with the Sopwith Aviation Company, of

Below: "Supercharging," W.O. Bentley is reputed to have said, "is a perversion of design. If you want more power, build a bigger engine." Most motorcycle designers seem to have agreed with him: supercharged and turbocharged motorcycles have never achieved wide acceptance, even in racing, with few exceptions such as this 1939 Manx Senior T.T. BMW.

Above: *The famous blue-and-white BMW roundel is supposed to relate to the aero-engine ancestry of the Bayerische Motoren Werke; it represents a propeller spinning against a blue sky.*

Sopwith Camel fame, who actually built the machine), the ABC
survived in France until 1924 in both 400cc and 500cc guises.
There, it was built by another aviation company, Gnome et Rhone.

The ultimate flat-twin, then or since, was, however, made in
Germany. As a former supplier of aero engines to the Kaiser, who
had recently stopped buying, the Bayerische Motoren Werke was
desperate for something to make. In 1923 they introduced a shaft-
driven motorcycle, the R32, with a 500cc (actually 494cc, 68mm
"square") unit-construction engine. The power output was a very
modest 8.5 bhp, but it could still propel the 264-lb. (120kg)
motorcycle at up to about 100 kph (62 mph). The tank was still
under the top tube – no saddle tanks here – and the overall look was
somewhat old-fashioned (as indeed some might say BMWs still
are today).

From that initial machine, of which 3100 were made, until the
present day, just about every BMW has been eligible for classic
status, though the bigger, faster machines inevitably steal the
limelight when compared with the smaller ones. The R32 commands
classic status because it was the first transverse BMW twin. The
R37 of 1925 was the first overhead-valve BMW; with that, and an
increased compression ratio, it delivered almost twice as much
power (16 bhp) as the R32 at somewhat higher revs; and it could
top 70 mph with ease, to say nothing of the vastly improved
acceleration. Then, in quick succession, there were faster side-
valve 500s (the R42) and much more powerful 750s: the side-valve

A SENIOR T.T. WINNER

R62 (1928, 18 bhp) and overhead-valve R63 (1928, 24 bhp). Just look at those figures a moment: from 8.5 bhp to 16 bhp to 24 bhp in five years!

Thereafter, you could take your pick of what constituted a "classic". The "star" model R11 side-valve with its pressed-steel frame? The R17 of 1935, with 33 bhp from 734cc and a top speed of 140 kph (near enough 87 mph)? The R5 of 1936, the first BMW with a foot change instead of a hand-lever? The R51 (500cc) and R61 (600cc) of 1938, with rear suspension? Even the single-cylinder BMWs, made from 1925 (the 6.5 bhp R39) to 1967 (the year the R27 died, 18 bhp and all)? The BMW will reappear in every chapter in this book; never were they the fastest production motorcycles ever made, and they even had a few rivals for sheer quality (Brough, Vincent, Hesketh), but they have a mystique all their own.

During the 1930s, even Douglas went over from the fore-and-aft flat twin to the transverse twin, with the Endeavour (a 500cc side-valve unit with shaft drive), and this has to be another classic. All of the designs already mentioned, though, were about to be eclipsed by one which had hitherto been of very modest importance, the parallel twin. The original 650cc Triumph Twin of 1935 is arguably a classic, but its post-war derivatives were to preside over both the greatest days of British motorcycles, and the worst.

Below: *The Ace Motor Corporation of Philadelphia was founded by Bill Henderson of Henderson motorcycle fame. He was killed in 1922, the year before* this "racer" was made. It was a nice 'bike, but big and heavy; even with four cylinders (and a single carburettor) it was out of the mainstream of racing.

Above: *Although it was a well-finished machine, and quick enough for a side-valve single of modest capacity, this 1922 Triumph Model SD was definitely "everyman" rather than "superman," or "transport" rather than "sport." And when saddle tanks caught on in the next half-decade, it suddenly looked very old-fashioned indeed. Its bicycle-style front brake and external contracting-band rear brake did nothing to make it look any more modern.*

Left: *To this day there are many motorcyclists for whom there is only one real race in the whole world: the Isle of Man Tourist Trophy. Any manufacturer who could advertise "A Senior T.T. Winner" (as Norton could for many years, and did here in the 1930s) gained great prestige.*

Everyman *and* Superman

Above: *This 1928 Vincent/H.R.D. Meteor is visibly the ancestor of the Comet single and its immortal V-twin derivative, the Rapide/ Shadow/Lightning, though it has surprisingly little in common with them. The "H.R.D" stands for H.R. Davis; Phil Vincent bought the company late in 1928, and this machine must be one of the last before Vincent started fitting his own unique suspension. Before 1935, Vincent/H.R.D. machines used bought-in J.A.P. engines.*

Right: *The prewar, overhead-cam 248cc Excelsior Manxman was a beautiful machine, a little heavy for its power potential but blessed with excellent roadholding and reliability. Like the bigger Norton singles, it went on winning races long after it should in theory have become uncompetitive. In 1933 another Excelsior had won the Lightweight T.T.: the "Mechanical Marvel," ridden by Sid Gleave. Postwar Excelsiors were boring two-strokes.*

Left: *Exposed valve gear on this 1930 T.T. Rudge probably improved cooling, but it did nothing for valve longevity – though in an era when "decokes" were routine maintenance, maybe this did not matter so much. What is more interesting is that this is a 4-valve head; count the exhaust pipes ….*

Right: *To this day Moto Guzzis enjoy a reputation for impeccable handling; pretty much as they always have done, ever since they introduced their first "flat single" (with the cylinder parallel with the ground). This handsome, deep-red racer, with the Guzzi trademark "bacon slicer" external flywheel, dates from the 1930s.*

3

CLASSICS
and
CLUNKERS

Above: *The gleaming, black-enamelled crank case of the magnificent Vincent Black Shadow.* Main picture: *a 1954 BSA Gold Flash.*

CLASSICS and CLUNKERS

ORLD WAR TWO stifled motorcycle development for a long time. It killed a number of makers outright, mostly firms that went over to producing war matériel and then never switched back to making motorcycles: Brough Superior was the greatest casualty in this class, though many component manufacturers also disappeared. Some, of course, were literally killed by the bombing of the Midlands, where so many of them were based.

There were great bikes from the immediately pre-war years, and even some from the wartime years, but most (though not all) of them had to wait until well after the war for development and widespread popularity. This chapter covers the period from the eve of the Second World War to the late 1950s; in my view, the Golden Age of motorcycling.

Everyone has his own idea of when the "Golden Age" of motorcycling was; some say the 1920s, some say the 1930s, some say the 1940s and 1950s. Probably, a lot depends on your age: the motorcycles of your adolescence are the ones that you value most highly. Remember, though, that the motorcycles of one's adolescence are a strange mixture: you read about the latest and the fastest, but usually ride machines that are anything from a couple of years to a couple of decades old, so (for example) anyone whose riding career started in the 1960s would almost certainly have been

Below: About 80,000 WL-series Harleys were made during World War Two; all featured the 45 cid (750cc) flat-head engine. Many were recycled into civilian use, and survive to this day.

Right: The Norton 16H in War Department trim looked like a piece of military machinery in its dull, threatening olive drab, angular accessories, and no hint of frippery anywhere.

familiar with the machines of the 1950s. On top of all this, there are always holdovers from the past: apart from the disk brakes and the electric starter, a BMW of the mid-1970s would not have seemed that unfamiliar to a BMW owner from the mid-1950s. Arguably, every age of motorcycling is a golden age: it just depends on what you want.

But consider this. By the eve of World War Two, you could buy fast, sweet-handling, reliable motorcycles with foot-operated gear changes and suspension at both ends. They were simple enough that almost anyone with any pretensions to being mechanically minded could understand them and work on them; indeed, some of the greatest among them, like the HRD (Vincent) for example, were specifically designed to be easy to work on, with no special "factory tools." With the right combination of preventive maintenance and periodical rebuilds, just about every motorcycle you could buy could be made to last half way to forever. Spares were readily available, because few if any of the dozens of manufacturers who existed world-wide had cottoned on to the "dispose-a-bike" spares philosophy. Throughout the 1950s, this trend continued. If that isn't a golden age, what is?

It is true that there were flies in the ointment. Not for nothing was Joe Lucas called "the Prince of Darkness," and Miller electrics were, if anything, worse; and with six-volt systems, even the best

Below: *Now refinished in more handsome and traditional Indian livery, this 45 cid (750cc) with its hand change and foot clutch would have looked very dull and drab in 1945. This big, heavy motorcycle had a low-compression version of the old faithful V-twin, and slightly increased ground clearance. It was deadly slow, but virtually indestructible.*

1942 Indian (Model 741B)

Outfitted for Royal Air Force police duties, this Indian 741B is much more handsome than its army counterparts – but no more modern. Unlike Harley-Davidson, who made the WLC model with foot shift and hand clutch (most of the 20,000 WLCs went to the Canadians), Indian made no concession to the sensibilities of riders accustomed to what we would now call "conventional" motorcycles. The right-hand gearshift was complemented by a left-foot clutch, and the whole motorcycle weighed over 450 lb. Any unfortunate Briton who was ordered to ride such a dinosaur must have wished for a Norton 16H or any other modern motorcycle.

The 1942 model year saw the 30.5 cid (500cc) Model 640, and the 45 cid (750cc) Model 741. Although today these are prized collectors' items, for many, many years after World War Two they were a drag on the market.

This is very much a civilian motorcycle that has been lightly militarized; just look at all the lights. The white crash bars, polished engine cases and carefully applied R.A.F. roundels and insignia are almost stylish for a military machine.

The leather saddlebags with their triple buckles are a feature that many modern riders would love to emulate, and the painted, spoked wheels look as if they could go anywhere. The whole thing has the macho charm of a modern Paris-Dakar replica.

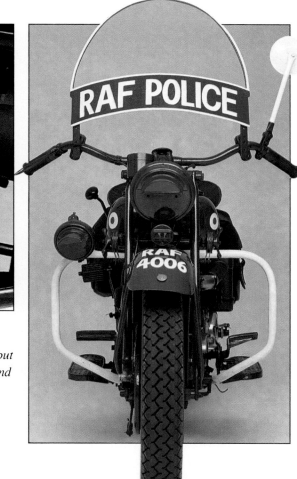

Details abound: the grease nipple on the front of the seat hinge, the stamped instructions on the air cleaner.

The lights may be of the regulation "blackout" pattern, but there are plenty of them, front and rear.

A vast, oiled-wire air cleaner fed a tiny carburettor: dust in the works was not a problem for military motorcyclists. The weird

clutch-actuating mechanism can clearly be seen; a hand clutch lever would have required a gorilla to work it.

For solo use, the tyres were inflated only to modest pressures ("TP 18" is 18 psi); this gave a soft ride and good traction. Add to

this the big saddle, and it is clear that the rider could at least be comfortable.

electrics were not too good. At best, with the charging and ignition systems working perfectly, pre-QI (quartz-iodine) headlamps did little to light the way ahead at night. Starting was strictly by kick: the electric foot had been tried (by Indian) as long ago as 1914, but it had never really caught on. By modern standards, power outputs were laughably low: 30 to 40 bhp was a fast motorcycle, 40 to 50 bhp was a superbike, and anything much more than that was outrageous. The legendary Black Lightning could boast only 70 bhp. And, as mentioned elsewhere, brakes were not always impressive: the ones that stopped you fastest were also the ones that took longest to set up, as anyone who has ever fiddled with the myriad adjustments of a four-leading-shoe drum will tell you. Then again, top speeds were low: the magic "ton" (100 mph) was still out of reach of all but the fastest motorcycles until the mid-to-late 1950s.

As it happens, though, you can still buy motorcycles that are essentially 1950s in spirit (most notably Harley Davidson, but arguably also BMW "boxers"), or whose design actually does date from the 1950s (Indian Enfield, or the "BMWski" Urals, Dneiprs and Cossacks from the Soviet Union); and, of course, enough motorcycles from the 1950s survive that many motorcyclists will have had the opportunity of riding them; something which is much less likely to be the case with machines dating from the first half of the century. You can therefore judge for yourself whether it truly was a "golden age," or whether you would rather have a much faster, much more reliable, much more oil-tight modern machine. The drawbacks to the modern motorcycle, unfortunately, are that the average rider simply cannot do more than the most basic maintenance; that the machine is normally designed for ease and

Left: *The post-war P&M (Phelon and Moore)/Panther line consisted of big, long-stroke singles where the engine formed the front down-tube of the frame. The "Big Pussy" was popular for hauling sidecars, but went out of production in 1965.*

Below: *The Velocette LE – here seen in its Mk. III, 200cc form dating from 1960 – was introduced in 1948 and remained in production for over a quarter of a century. It was an incredibly reliable, very comfortable, extremely economical, superbly-*

handling and utterly bizarre motorcycle which combined old (side-valves), new (liquid cooling), and a good measure of total originality. Apart from its looks, which have a weird charm of their own, its chief defect was that it was dog-slow.

Left: *The Panther Model 100 was blessed with an 87mm x 100mm single-cylinder engine of 589cc. The "big brother" Model 120 increased the bore by 1mm and the stroke by 6mm for 645cc and immense torque – but it was a very old-fashioned engine.*

Below: *The shape of things to come: a dohc Honda 4-cylinder 250cc racer from 1959 or 1960. Small fours were nothing new, but Honda made them reliable enough to win races – and then based roadgoing motorcycles on their racers.*

economy of *production* rather than for ease of *maintenance*; and that almost all modern motorcycles are designed to be replaced after a few years rather than to be kept running.

It is also with the 1950s that the distinction between "cooking" and "classic" motorcycles becomes most obvious. Anyone over the age of, say, 40 can recall consigning to the scrap-heap machines which today would be called "classics" and which would command spectacular prices. The *real* classics, such as the Vincents and MV Agustas and Manx Nortons and BSA Gold Stars and AJS 7Rs were always classics and recognized as such; but (for example) most Royal Enfield singles (especially the 350s) were dismissed as pretty ordinary, and even the big Enfield twins were regarded as seriously flawed, because they used to break if you went too fast. The lovely Sunbeam S7 and S8 were callously dismissed as "slugs." The monster old long-stroke Panther singles, the "Big Pussies," were old men's motorcycles, normally seen in a broken-down state towing improbably-huge, Watsonian double-adult sidecars. The BSA Bantam was a joke (it still is). The list of motorcycles that no-one loved (or not enough people loved) could be continued indefinitely: the Velocette LE-series "Noddy bikes," almost anything with a Villiers or AMC two-stroke motor, the smaller Ariels, the last gasps of makers like NSU before they became makers of mopeds or at best tiresome lightweights.

To be fair, there are still many machines from this era that are even now regarded as trash, and justly so: the Ariel Leader is as ugly and sluggish now as it was when it was introduced in 1957, though its styling does have a certain 1950s kitsch appeal. In fact, most 250s from British manufacturers were gruesome: the BSA C15, the Norton Jubilee.

1949 Triumph 6T

T HE TRIUMPH 6T IS very close to the Speed Twin of 1937: the motorcycle that killed the British motorcycle industry. The 500cc overhead-valve parallel twin was so good, so powerful, so reliable, and so cheap to make that it was almost impossible for anything else to compete – so innovation died. This type of machine would define motorcycling for a third of a century or so. The only real problems came from increasing vibration as the swept volume increased: this was what led to the adoption of in-line fours, and the return of the V-twin.

The luggage rack on the tank was at first sight an excellent idea, but after a few unfortunate accidents people saw the unwisdom of having a strong, rigidly-mounted rack just forward of the rider's legs. The feature was dropped, never to reappear, though police motorcycles sometimes had a cubby-hole in the tank, or a telephone on it.

A parallel twin has to be compared with what it replaced: essentially, the 500cc single. At 500cc, the twin is remarkably adaptable and one basic engine design can be configured in a number of ways, which is a manufacturer's dream. If you want torque and reliability, fit a single carburettor, mild cams and leave the compression ratio low. It will be smoother and more powerful than any comparable single. For a fast roadster, put one carburettor on each cylinder, make the cams lumpier, and skim the head, and you will see off any but a full-race single. Just don't go much bigger than 500cc; the 828cc Norton Commando is an object lesson in how not to make parallel twins.

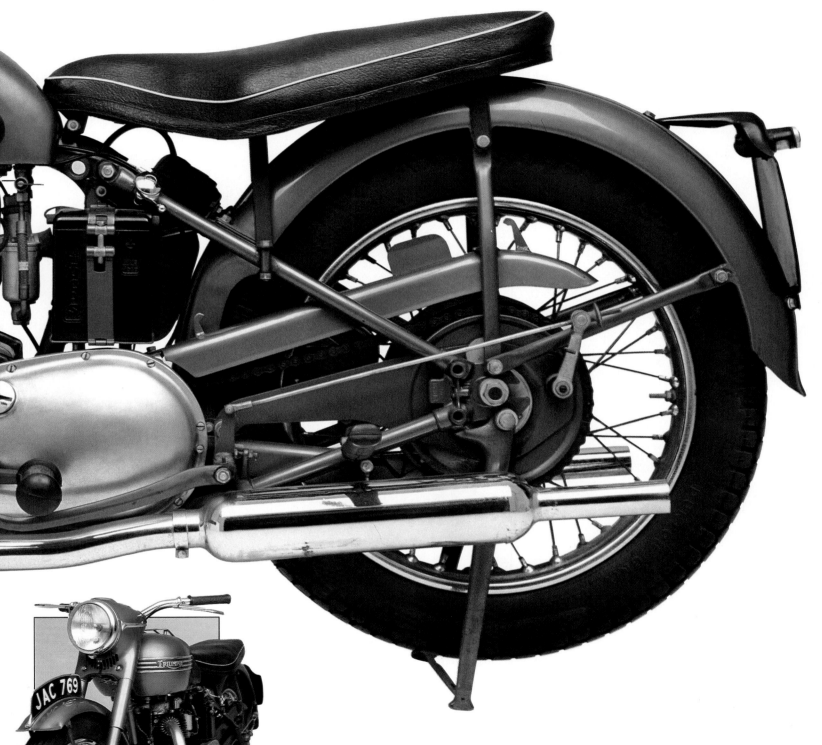

There are many motorcyclists who believe that two cylinders is the optimum number for a motorcycle. A single cylinder delivers too little power and too much vibration, while any more than two cylinders means too much weight and too much complication. The only argument is how the cylinders should be disposed, and BMW, Harley, and Moto-Guzzi riders all have their own opinions. But even they have to admit that for simplicity and elegance, the parallel twin is hard to beat. It is also a question of aesthetics: next to a twin, a four-valve single looks ill-proportioned, and a triple (or more) looks gross.

Left: *Tank-mounted instruments on this 1947 Squariel show strong American influence, but the complex engine was totally unsuitable for the American market, which was used to big, crude V-twins and which could not maintain anything else.*

Right: *Daytona Beach really is a beach, and it makes a wonderful backdrop for photographing Harleys. If looks are the criterion – and it certainly isn't performance – then the old white flathead on the left is the winner, in my considered opinion.*

The 1950s were also the decade when Europeans first became aware of the Honda Motor Company, principally as manufacturers of startlingly-ugly, small motorcycles with startlingly-powerful engines. Although Soichiro Honda had set up shop in Hammamatsu in 1946, the first Honda twin was the Dream 250 of 1957.

Perhaps the greatest thing about this era, though, was these sheer variety of machines that were available. About the only format that did not make it into series production was the triple. The air-cooled longitudinal four survived (just) in the Nimbus, as described in the last chapter. The transverse four appeared for the first time in a road-going machine in the MV-Agusta. The square four soldiered on in the Ariel, and there was the utterly improbable Wooler flat four which never made serious production. The V-twin was most nobly represented by the Vincent, though Indian survived on its last legs and Harley-Davidson plodded on. Transverse flat twins came from BMW (as always), from various BMW imitators (such as Condor) and from Douglas and Velocette. Singles came in a bewildering variety of shapes, cylinder angles, sizes and degrees of sportiness, including "split single" two-strokes with a pumping cylinder and a combustion cylinder; and the parallel twin bid fair to overcome them all.

The longitudinal four can be quickly dismissed; the overhead-cam Nimbus was a classic, but an eccentric one. The 600cc transverse four MV Agusta was a foretaste of things to come, but with its shattering price tag and its very limited production numbers, it was not a mainstream machine. Although it was one of the most desirable machines in the world from the instant it was introduced, most motorcyclists to this day have never even *seen* one. If they have, it was almost certainly in a museum. The Squariel, meanwhile, was a leftover from a bygone age (even if the engine was all-alloy from 1949) and the Wooler was not the obvious Volkswagen or Honda Goldwing style of flat four, but had a horrifically complex bottom end in which a single-throw crankshaft was operated by a bell-crank coupled to all four cylinders ….

The V-twin, too, seemed to be on the way out. During the War, American flat-head 45s (45 cid = 750cc) had done sterling service, but they were hardly of a technical specification to excite a European buyer: big, heavy, crude and sluggish, they would last forever but that was about all you could say for them, except, to be fair, that they looked and sounded like motorcycles, which is always useful.

Many other V-twin manufacturers had simply gone under. J.A.P. was still making tiny numbers of engines for assemblers, but their heart was not in it; they had been taken over (O ignominy!) by Villiers. The Harley-Davidson Knucklehead was at least a decade behind the times even when it was introduced, and appeared to have survived only because the American market was positively Neanderthal in its demands for technological sophistication. Only

Left: *The Ariel Square Four in all-alloy form was more powerful and better-cooled than the original (this is a 1953 Mk II), but it was still a motorcycle in search of a market. It had torque, and it could reach high speeds if you did not want to sustain them (the rear cylinders overheated); but the European market for big, heavy tourers was never large, and as average speeds rose, the Squariel's desirability fell.*

Above: *There have always been some motorcycles which were effectively street-legal racers – or alternatively, racers which could be made street-legal. The "Goldie" was one, and the MV Agusta transverse fours were a much more modern version of the same thing; they were the first transverse fours to enter regular production. This 500 dates from 1954 or 1955 and is Lucio Castelli's bike.*

Left: *You can tell that this Vincent is a Rapide, and not a Shadow, from the polished crank-cases instead of the black enamel. This is a 1952 model, in the eyes of many the zenith of Vincent production before financial problems beset the company too badly.*

Right: *The Vincent Black Shadow has been described as a huge engine to which were bolted the bare minimum of parts necessary to make a motorcycle. With its massive, black-enamelled crank cases and its plethora of polished alloy and chrome, it is utterly beautiful.*

the HRD Vincent, introduced in 1936 as the Series A "Plumber's Nightmare" (of which only 78 were made) and substantially redesigned during the war for post-war production as the Series B, was a real classic.

The story of the birth of the Vincent, the result of the accidental overlapping of two blueprints for the Comet 500 single and the resulting "what if ...?" is true. The prototype was built with an included angle of 47.5-degrees, for no better reason than that it had to fit into a frame that a customer had ordered (for a J.A.P. engine) and then not collected; the angle remained for the Series A. The external oil pipes, and a few other details, were cleaned up in the Series B, while the cylinder angle was increased to 50-degrees, and the Series B "frame" consisted in large part of the massive engine, which was a stressed member. All Vincent V-twin frames were literally hinged in the middle: instead of a swinging arm, the whole back end of the motorcycle swings, resulting in an initially-disconcerting, up-and-down movement of the back of the seat.

The basic Rapides, both Series A and Series B, offered a modest 45 bhp. This figure, laughably low by modern standards, would get a Series A up to an easy 100 mph, and a Series B was a little faster. But Philip Irving, the company's chief designer, and Philip Vincent wanted a *fast* Vincent twin, so they had two Rapides built up with Comet cams, compression ratios of 7.3:1 (the Rapide ran at 6.5:1

because of the poor "pool" petrol of the time), and spectacular, black-enamelled engine cases. The standard 120 mph speedometer was replaced with a five-inch diameter, 150 mph "clock." The result was the Black Shadow, which could hit 120 mph almost anywhere if it was in good condition and which could just about achieve 125 mph (a whisker over the 200 kph mark) at full stretch. All this from only 55 bhp! Ah, they had bigger horses in those days.

The Series C, which ran from 1948 to 1955 inclusive, had detail changes and was one of the top ten motorcycles of all time; in the estimation of many, the top motorcycle of all time. Almost all road testers managed to hit, and sometimes comfortably to exceed, 200 kph (124 mph).

Also in 1948, the Black Lightning was introduced: bristling with "added lightness," the Lightning weighed under 400 pounds and boasted 70 bhp. It was a production motorcycle, and could exceed 140 mph on a regular basis; Rollie Free managed to exceed 150 mph in a (successful) attempt on the motorcycle speed record, though at the time he was lying full length on the saddle and wearing only shorts and running shoes! The Lightning was not intended as a roadgoing motorcycle, but a few Lightning-spec motors did appear in street-legal bikes.

Finally, there was the Black Knight, an all-enclosed machine which rarely looks good in pictures but which is surpassingly

Left: *The R69S (1960-1969) was the last of the "old" BMWs before the engine and frame were completely redesigned for the new 5 series: many find its lines irresistible. A few heretics have however put the newer, more reliable and even more handsome modern engines into these frames. The R69US (for the American market) had tele forks instead of Earles.*

Right: *Fewer and fewer people get the opportunity actually to ride a Vincent, as the prices rise further and further into the investment stratosphere; but when you do get the chance, the experience is unforgettable. And some heroes actually race these all but priceless motorcycles!*

1955 Vincent "BLACK PRINCE"

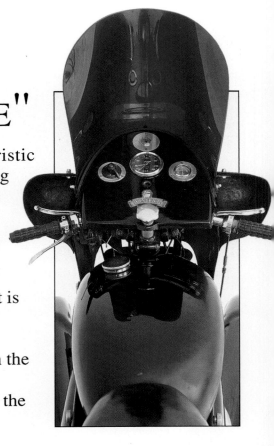

THE BLACK PRINCE WAS a Black Shadow with remarkably futuristic bodywork, introduced in 1954; this is a 1955 model. Part of the fairing has been removed to expose the engine more fully; with the Rapide engine, the same machine would have been a Black Knight.

The intention was to create a machine with excellent weather protection, which would also be very easy to clean; both goals were achieved handsomely. The beautifully-finished black fibreglass bodywork was originally complemented by a clear screen, rather than a smoked one like this, and it is disputable which is more attractive.

Neither the Black Prince nor the Black Knight was a great success, however. The design was a little too futuristic for most motorcyclists with the money to buy such a machine, and besides, the financial troubles which would sink Vincent were all too evident. This 1955 Series D was made in the last year that Vincent was in business.

The Thought Police rode fully-faired Vincents in the original movie version of George Orwell's 1984; it had a sort of sinister, futuristic elegance which suited their trade well. It was another regime that finished the Vincent, though; a large order of motorcycles for the Argentine police fell through, and Argentine currency regulations prevented Phil Vincent's father (who was a wealthy rancher in Argentina) from bailing the company out. At least, that's the legend.

The Series D was "de-specced" somewhat when compared with earlier Vincents – instant, tommy-bar removal of the wheels was sacrificed, for instance, in order to reduce costs – but (for example) the centre stand was operated by pulling up on a long hand lever which normally lay parallel with the ground, along the lower edge of the left side of the fairing.

CLASSICS and CLUNKERS

Left and below: *The Wehrmacht bought 16,500 R75s. They were massive, improbable sidecar machines with a two-speed high/low ratio gearbox to complement the 4-speed-plus-reverse (!) main box, and a separate drive to the sidecar, complete with lockable differential and hydraulic brakes. The downrated 750cc ohv engine delivered only 26 bhp (albeit with plenty of torque), and the unladen outfit weighed 420 Kg (924 lb).*

lovely in real life. Alas, PCV was always more of an enthusiast than a businessman: that, and several strokes of bad luck, killed the Series D Rapide in 1955, though the the last Vincent was actually "de-specced" compared with earlier machines.

Although the Vincent was wonderful, it was not perfect. The biggest single fault was the clutch. The bought-in, pre-war unit was not man enough for the job (nor was the gearbox), so the Series B sported a self-servo clutch, an ingenious invention which allowed two-finger clutch operation on a very powerful motorcycle (the gearbox was also vastly improved). The trouble was, the oil seals in the clutch sometimes leaked; and when they did, clutch slip ensued rapidly, convincingly, and depressingly. Also, unless you were careful and experienced in the starting drill, you ran the risk of a terrifying kick-back which has been known to break ankles and to throw riders over low walls. This is one of the reasons why electric starters are *de rigueur* with so many modern, powerful bikes: it would be nearly impossible to kick over (say) a Hesketh.

As for the flat twin, BMW had settled into being solid, reliable motorcycles for gentlemen who wanted to travel very long distances in considerable comfort at very respectable speeds, but who were not concerned with being either the fastest or the most dramatic machines on the road. Not until the 590cc R69 of 1955 did BMW build a machine with a catalogued speed of more than 100 mph. In all fairness, the 165 kph (102.3 mph) advertised speed was probably lower than the true speed, but it was still well behind, say, a Vincent; and the R69 was the fastest production BMW made until 1969! The Earles front forks looked odd, but worked. Are these machines classics? Many would say so, but they were beautifully-made classics rather than exciting classics. Also, like the Vincent, they had their faults. You needed to be generous with the oil changes, and you had to *ride* the motorcycle; infrequent riders, or those who neglected lubrication, sometimes found that sludge build-up might cause big-end failure at as little as 40,000 miles. The "plunger" ignition key was prone to corrosion, and rapid riding on back-roads was not the older Beemers' *forte*; there was distressingly little road feel.

There were some very entertaining wartime BMWs, including the incredible outfit with the ancillary drive to the sidecar wheel; though no doubt they are more entertaining today than they were if you were forced to ride them in the Wehrmacht. These things still surface from time to time, or you may still be able to buy a new Russian copy, which is a pastiche of BMW design from about 1935 to 1955. With the right rider, such a machine is all but unstoppable; most people find that their nerve gives out long before the outfit refuses an obstacle. The Russian solo twins have a certain perverse charm, too, but they need various parts replaced (such as valves, for example) before they can be considered reliable. This book was

Below: *The Douglas Mk V of 1951 was much like a smaller, lighter, more sporting and more technically advanced BMW. The finish was as good, too, but the bike was somewhat less reliable.*

Right: *Early "Douggies" mounted their flat twins in line with the chassis, and some saw service in World War Two; but in 1935 they changed to transverse mounting. This is the 1951 Mk V.*

Left and right: *Ingenious suspension was a hallmark of Douggies – they even used torsion bars – but unlike BMWs they had chain final drive; the right-angle in the drive train was shifted forward.*

CLASSICS and CLUNKERS

written in the early 1990s, and it looked as if the Russian machines were rapidly heading for classic status in the sense that they would probably go out of production in the near future.

Two other transverse-twin classics were the Douglases and Velocettes, two machines which could hardly have been less alike.

The Douggies were like much smaller, lighter, nimbler BMWs, which embraced such improbable technical features as torsion-bar suspension. The 90 Plus was introduced in 1949 as a racer which could be (and usually was) made street legal; the number referred to the maximum speed, just like the old Broughs, but remember that this was a 344cc machine; and works versions, using components that were also available to privateers, exceeded 100 mph (one was timed at 108.4 mph, as near as makes no odds 175 kph, on the Island). The road-going version, sold complete with headlights and a wider-ratio gearbox, was the 80 Plus. The Dragonfly of 1954 was a development of the same bike, with somewhat eccentric styling and putrid coloured paint; but I would still say that any Douggie was a classic, even if they did crack frames and shed bits.

According classic status to the baby Velocettes will invite more dispute. The original side-valve flat twin Velocette LE 150 of 1948 could hardly have been further from the classic singles for which the firm was renowned. Nor was it fast: the 148cc engine could barely drag the machine above 40 mph. There was a hand-starter, and a hand gearchange; it must surely have been the last all-new bike to feature the latter. And when it came to styling, it looked like a biscuit-tin built in a shipyard, an improbable, angular brute with acres of flat metal everywhere. It was water-cooled, offered a considerable measure of weather protection (leg shields

Left: *The 348cc Douglas Dragonfly was just about the last gasp of the Bristol factory (they ceased production in 1956), and pea-soup green was a standard color. This is a classic touring rig, with a Steib sidecar painted (and lettered!) to match, and the quadrant panniers which were hard to pack but were very comfortable for the passenger.*

Above: *Royal Enfield singles were made as 350s and 500s, and as the softer-tuned "Clipper" or the faster "Bullet." This is a 1951 Bullet 350, regarded as a rather ordinary motorcycle in its time, but now achieving minor classic status. A firm in Bristol, L&D Motors, can still supply just about all you need to keep your Enfield running.*

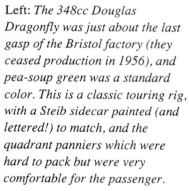

Left: *The Velocette Valiant (this one dates from 1958) was an air-cooled, ohv version of the LE 200 engine in a conventional frame. It was sweet-handling and hopelessly underpowered, but looks gorgeous in classic Velocette black.*

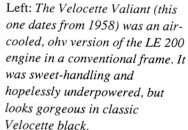

Right: *The 1963 Rocket Gold Star was a good motorcycle which suffered from being given the classic Gold Star appellation when the original Goldie single went out of production. Purists shunned it, and ignoramuses took their lead from the purists.*

1958 AJS 7R

UNIVERSALLY KNOWN AS THE "Boy's Racer," the AJS 7R was introduced in 1948/49 and was one of the most desirable 350cc singles of all time. The "boy's" appellation came from its being only a 350cc motorcycle (the "Junior") formula, and racer it most certainly was, with perfect road manners and as much power as you could decently ask for from a 350cc single. The "bacon slicer" cooler on the front brake may or may not have had much effect on cooling, but it became a standard styling cue for "café racer" motorcycles, as did the "bum-stop" seat, the clip-on bars and the rear-set footrests with reversed gear-lever and abbreviated rear brake lever.

Air filtration would have been utterly contrary to the spirit of the Boy's Racer; a ram stack might admit moths, dust, spiders and even small stones, but it allowed the carburettor to breathe deeply *and easily. A backfire – by no means unlikely, even with run-and-bump starting – meant a spectacular blast of flame, fortunately directed away from the rider.*

A megaphone exhaust; big, conical brakes with "turbo" cooling slots; no provision for number plates or lighting; no kick-start; a chin-pad on the tank for tucking behind the fly-screen; no speedometer, just a rev counter; exposed, ventilated primary drive; the closer you look at this motorcycle, the more there is to see. This is a racer, pure and simple, but it was a racer that many clubmen could actually afford.

A.J.S. grew out of Joe Stevens's Stevens Screw Co. Ltd in Wolverhampton, where engines were being built as early as 1897. Joe was blessed with four sons, Harry, George, Jack and Joe, and they built the first A.J.S. motorcycle in 1909.
For over two decades they raced and won, and they sold motorcycles, but in 1931 the depression moved the Stevens brothers to sell out to the Collier brothers, who made Matchlesses in London. This was the foundation of A.M.C., Associated Motorcycles, who after the war also acquired James, Francis-Barnett and even Norton. That such magical motorcycles could emerge from such an unwieldy and often complacent consortium is little short of a miracle.

and a big windscreen), and was almost impossible to "lose," because the engine would not propel it fast enough to go outside its safe handling envelope. The police bought them as urban patrol bikes, allegedly because they were so quiet (actually, they are not too remarkable in that department), but no-one else loved them very much.

Later LEs (it stands for "Little Engine") eventually grew to 200cc, and acquired conventional foot changes and kick-starters, though the kick starter was still so gentle that it could be operated by hand. For all the LE's eccentricities, it was (and is) a delightful bike to ride; the perfect town bike, vastly more fun than any moped, scooterette, step-through or anything else built since. It really is a classic, albeit an eccentric one.

Meanwhile, Velocette also decided to make an overhead-valve version of the LE, but with air cooling and a more conventional appearance. Widely derided during its production life – after all, who *needs* a 200cc micro-BMW? – it now attracts an understandable amount of collectors' attention as an improbable aberration from one of the greatest manufacturers of all time. It shared shaft drive with the LE, and was very nearly as simple and reliable. Certainly, it is more of a ridable classic than some ostensibly more glamorous lightweights, such as early Ducatis or baby Guzzis.

Single-cylinder motorcycles were by now in an anomalous position. Effectively, they had divided into two branches: straightforward (but often very agreeable) basic transport, and remarkably quick sports bikes.

Even the "transport" bikes are now widely regarded as classics in many cases. Machines like the Royal Enfield 500 Bullet have a timeless charm which allows one to forget the *very* low power outputs, roughly equivalent to a modern 175cc or 200cc machine. The 350cc versions of the same machines are every bit as pleasant,

Above: *The "brain-bucket" helmet may be anachronistic – compressed-cork "piss-pot" helmets were the thing in the days when AJS 7Rs were first raced – but the old "Boy's Racer" still regularly gives a good account of itself. Peter Marriot is in the saddle of this 1956 model.*

Below: *The Manx Norton was the final development of the "cammy" 500cc single: eventually, they managed to extract 52 bhp at 7,000 rpm. But, with exactly the same piston speed, an MV Agusta 500 four could deliver 70 bhp at 10,500 rpm …. Tony Godfrey rides a 1955 Manx in this shot.*

until you start to ride them; then, power outputs of under 20 bhp (sometimes well under) will leave the rider wishing for more *oomph*. And when you go under 350cc, the traditional minimum size for a "boys' bike," most motorcycles from this period are suitable only for riding around town or for very modest journeys. This is not to deny that many people have happily toured on them; it is simply to state that today you may find them sadly underpowered. With the exception of the Velocettes mentioned above, and possibly some scooters, "Golden Age" lightweights were not all that golden.

The sports bikes were another matter. All of them benefited from at least a decade of development, often well beyond what any rational person could have expected. By rights, multi-cylinder machines should have begun to take over in any races that counted, including the Island; but the incredible thing was that the singles were so reliable, so refined, so close to perfection, that they just kept on winning.

The 500cc sporting single was also kept alive by club racing. Not only were singles affordable and fast; they were also easy to work on. All of the sports singles of the 1940s and 1950s are classics, though inevitably some are more classic than others. The Vincent Comet, for example, inevitably suffers from comparison with the twins; but the BSA Gold Star, developed continuously from its 1938 introduction to its demise in 1962, was one of the greatest singles ever. With about 38 to 40 bhp (at 7000 rpm!) and a dry weight of 350 pounds, it was virtually a racer on the road. In particular, the racing carburetter would foul the plugs at anything much less than three-quarter throttle, so the loud tap had to be blipped at frequent intervals to stop the engine dying in traffic. Taken with an exhaust note that could rattle windows, this meant that the Goldie was *not* a low-profile motorcycle.

Above: *The equation was unanswerable. Nortons handled like a dream, and cornered like ball-bearings in a groove, but were slow. Triumphs were more powerful, but didn't handle as well. What could be more natural than to slot a Triumph engine into a Norton frame and make a Triton?*

Below: *If you were really serious about your Triton, you used an unpainted light-alloy tank, clip-ons, rear-sets, and a plank-like seat with a bum-stop. The owner of this beautiful example has also added late Norton forks with a disc brake.*

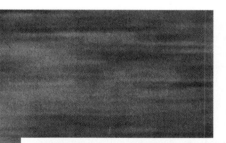

Below: *On this 1958 Manx Norton, finning encompasses the top of the cam drive tube as it progresses alongside the cylinder and head. With 100bhp per litre from an air-cooled single, heat dissipation causes problems.*

CLASSICS and CLUNKERS

Left: *The Norton "Dominator" series began with the Dommie 88; this is a 1959 Dommie 99 with less-than-original, but still stunning, paintwork. Even for 1959, though, there are certain touches which are beginning to look somewhat vintage, such as the non-unit gearbox and the single, small carburettor.*

Right: *The 650cc BSA A10, correctly the Golden Flash but always called the Gold Flash, was only one of many imitators of the Speed Twin/Thunderbird. Although this 1954 model might attract attention today, throughout the 1960s and 1970s it would have been dismissed as a cheap old dog; it would be a young man's first "real" bike.*

Above and left: *The original Triumph Speed Twin engine, first seen in 1937 (a 1939 model appears above), was very little bigger than the 493cc Tiger 90 single. It was an immediate success, and the post-war Thunderbird (left) was merely a 650cc version of the same machine with more power and vibration.*

It was, however, one of several super-sports singles. AJS introduced the 7R "Boy's Racer" (so called from its 350cc capacity) in 1948, and it instantly became a classic; the Manx and "Inter" Nortons continued from before the war, and the Matchless G50 was a 500cc development of the 7R. Then there were the Velocette 500cc singles, which would continue until the late 1960s.

Even so, the only matter of real technical novelty in these machines was the appearance of the Norton "featherbed" frame in the early 1950s: the engines were mere incremental developments of what had gone before. The handling and comfort of the

"featherbed" was so outstanding that it artificially extended the life of the old Norton singles by putting them at an enormous advantage on any course where handling was at least as important as sheer, raw power (which, of course, the Nortons did not have). Other manufacturers did their best to catch up, and although none ever quite succeeded, the frame was at least as much as the engine the key to the continuing success of the classic British single.

The McCandless-designed Featherbed was the basis for many, many specials where a fast engine was married to a fast frame. The original narrow-line could be persuaded to accept a good range of engines, and the later wide-line would accept almost anything. The all-time classics were the Triton (a Triumph engine in a Norton frame) and the Norvin (a Vincent engine in a Norton frame), but almost everything was tried at one time or another, including a number of Japanese offerings, and even the Hillman Imp car engine.

At the end of the last chapter, though, and earlier in this one, I said that we had come to the era of the parallel twin; and now it is time to switch our attention to that.

The basic premise of the parallel twin is simple: two small cylinders can be filled, ignited, and exhausted faster than one big one. If the engine is designed properly, the reciprocating masses (pistons and connecting rods) are less than they are for a single of comparable swept volume. And, to cap it all, if the pistons rise and fall together, there is a power stroke on every revolution, with firing intervals evenly spaced. You therefore get more power, more smoothly.

On the down side, a parallel twin is considerably more complicated to make, and is therefore more expensive. It also vibrates almost as badly as a single, because the pistons rise and fall together. Even so, it is clearly cheaper, lighter and simpler than a V-twin or a flat twin.

CLASSICS and CLUNKERS

The four-stroke parallel twin had been tried as early as the first decade of the century, but not until 1933 did an overhead valve version with a single-throw crankshaft appear in a production motorcycle: the Triumph 6/1. The motorcycle as a whole was nothing remarkable, but the engine was an omen for the future, and in 1937 (for the 1938 season) the Speed Twin came out.

It was a revelation: an easy 90 mph in stock trim, at a reasonable price from an established mass-market maker. At only 500cc, it was a small, light engine in a small, light frame, a logical descendant of the singles that had for so long dominated the British motorcycle scene. The intervention of World War Two meant that its imitators were delayed until the mid-to-late 1940s, but when they arrived, they rapidly became the standard. BSA introduced the A7, to be followed by Norton's Dominator; Ariel's Red Hunter; and others from AJS, Matchless and just about anyone else who stayed in business.

Almost immediately, the size began to rise from the original 500cc range; soon, 650cc was the norm, as exemplified by Triumph's own Thunderbird, BSA's Gold Flash, and Norton's eventual equivalent. It was generally agreed that 650cc was as big as you could go without running into serious vibration problems, and there were many who reckoned that even 650cc was too big, and that 500cc was more appropriate. Then came the 750s ....

The welter of names comes easily to the tongue: the BSA Super Rocket, the Triumph Tiger 110, the Norton Atlas, the Royal

Below: The tank was all backwards, the rev limit was ridiculously high, and who had ever heard of a successful 250cc parallel twin anyway? But the quality of the castings was indisputable, and this 1966 Honda 250 Dream could see off most 350s and many 500s.

Above and left: *The pre-Isolastic Norton Atlas (introduced 1963) attracts a strong following among those who never rode them before they were collectable. In the days when they were just cheap, reasonably quick second-hand bikes with good handling, they were also famous for jackhammer vibration and were regarded as more suited to short blasts than to prolonged cruising. The silver bike is a '67; the red, a '65.*

Right: *The Sunbeam S8 was a slightly more sporting version of the S7, introduced in 1950. The emphasis is on "slightly:" this was still no roadburner. It was the last new motorcycle from Sunbeam, 1912-1957: R.I.P.*

CLASSICS and CLUNKERS

Enfield Meteor (with its unconventional 700cc capacity, but still good for 100 mph in Super Meteor guise) and later the Constellation (the fastest of all classic British twins), the Rocket Gold Star (a Rocket engine in a "Goldie" frame), and more. They would go on well into the '60s, most of them, and several would see the '70s. A few would even see the '80s. But in the long run, they would be the victims of their own success: just as the single had given way to the twin, so would the twin give way to the four.

The twin would, however, remain the layout for many small motorcycles (350cc and below), especially given the Japanese talent for building very small, very quick twins with the kind of rev limits hitherto associated only with out-and-out racers. The first Honda twin, the wildly over-styled Honda Dream 250, appeared in 1957. Also, BMW would persist with the flat twin, and Harley-Davidson would persist with the V-twin; but both companies (and their devotees) always marched to their own drummers, so parallel twins would come and go as they went on in their own sweet way.

Before we leave the twin, we should pay brief homage to a 'bike which was *not* one of the crowd, namely the Sunbeam S7 and the more sporty S8. The oversquare 500cc engine was rubber mounted in the frame, but running the "wrong" way, fore and aft instead of transversely. While this made shaft drive much easier, it did nothing for cooling. As so often, the manufacturers appear to have intended the machine to be driven much slower than it *could* be driven, which is always a dangerous assumption to make when you are dealing with motorcyclists. The result, inevitably, was that young blades dismissed both the S7 and the S8 as old men's motorcycles; and as old men are nothing like so good a market for motorcycles as young ones (or as those who are trying to recapture their youth), it withered and died. Anyone who ever rode one would agree, though: they were classics.

Above: *The big Indian four bit the dust in the 1940s, though it had a remarkably modern look just before its demise. Complexity, cost, and the relatively low power outputs possible with an air-cooled in-line four, were the reasons for its passing.*

Right: *These two old classics make for an interesting comparison. The 1931 motorcycle in the foreground is more H.R.D. than Vincent, with a bought-in engine, but the 1949 Rapide in the background is much more Vincent than H.R.D.*

Above left: *Harley-Davidsons kept such options as foot clutches and hand changes for so long that it was possible to order a motorcycle which was decades, rather than years, out of date.*

Left: *The Corgi was designed as an air-deliverable transport for paratroopers, but the 98cc Villiers engine and two-speed 'box made it a useful civilian runabout or "motor scooter."*

Above: *MV Agustas are the Ferraris of the motorcycle world. Apart from being blood-red and Italian, they are technically advanced and somewhat temperamental. Astride Agustas*

like this 350/4, John Surtees won both the Senior and Junior T.T.s in 1958 and 1959, apart from winning his first Agusta senior in 1956 and taking 350cc and 500cc GP titles in 1958, 1959 and 1960.

Above: *If you are going to ride elderly Royal Enfield Bullets, as Bryan Amos is doing here, you ought to try to look the part: waxed-cotton Barbour suit, "piss-pot" helmet and Mark goggles. The shoes are in period (boots would be safer); the gloves are not.*

Above: *The International Six Days' Trial (I.S.D.T.) was instituted in 1913 and was the premier event in what we would now call "dual sport." This Royal Enfield of Don Morley's is a 1954 I.S.D.T. team bike.*

Left: *One 1961 fire-engine red Royal Enfield Air-flow would be unusual enough; if you knew the whereabouts of two of them, as photographer Don Morley did, it would be hard to resist trying to set up a photo session.*

Above: *This is the way the T.T. used to be: John Surtees blasting to victory in 1958 on an MV Agusta. Racing motorcycles and hard brick or stone walls are a dangerous combination, but this is true road racing.*

Below: *Side-car racing requires a special breed of passenger, with nerves of steel, who can jump about like a monkey to keep the outfit on the road. This is D. Dickinson and M. Brett on a BMW in 1967.*

4

DEATH
—and—
REBIRTH

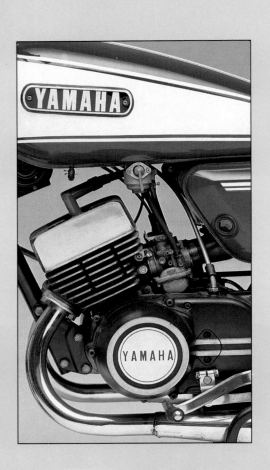

Above: *The Yamaha RD200 of 1972. Main picture: a Silk Scott from 1976.*

DEATH and REBIRTH

EDWARD TURNER, THE man responsible for the Speed Twin, visited Japan in 1960. In his report, he said "Japan has 90 million highly intelligent, very energetic, purposeful people, all geared to an economic machine with an avowed object of becoming great again, this time in the world of business and industry, and nothing apparently is going to stop them .... Although I will not be surprised to see less than 10 motorcycle companies in existence in three years' time, four or five of these 10 will be immensely powerful."

He could hardly have been more correct. All through the 1960s, British motorcycle manufacturers fell by the wayside; and Japanese manufacturers decreased in numbers, but greatly increased in puissance.

Ariel was dying on its feet, and with the ugly Arrow (a re-vamped Leader) the company finally went under in 1970. Phelon and Moore's Big Pussies finally chuffed to a halt in 1967. Royal Enfield made their last motorcycles fairly soon after. Velocette launched the Thruxton, arguably the last and greatest of British singles, in 1965, but it was their last gasp: they disappeared in 1968, though a few machines were assembled in the next couple of years or so. Also in 1968, the big AMC combine collapsed: goodbye to AJS/ Matchless, Frances Barnett (the Franny-Bee or Fanny-Bee) and James, though neither of the last two had made anything that was even close to a classic for decades.

None of these companies had introduced a genuinely new motorcycle for a very long time; indeed, many models in their line-up were firmly rooted in the days before World War Two. They had admittedly made some wonderful motorcycles, and there were still those who appreciated the utter purity of the Thruxton or the near indestructibility of a Royal Enfield single (which, unlike the Velo, had a reliable clutch). But in relative terms, British motorcycles were expensive, and motorcyclists were demanding more power than British manufacturers were apparently willing or able to provide.

Today, it is hard to see how these "classics" died: if they were still available today, then people would surely buy them. The answer is unfashionable, but indisputable: people are much wealthier

Above: *Today, anyone restoring a Velocette Thruxton would probably paint it black and gold; but as this mid-1960s shot shows, all kinds of other colours were once entirely acceptable and often attractive.*

Above right: *This is a 1966 model; the Thruxton was only in production from 1965 to 1968, when the company expired, but it is commonly (and with justice) called the last and greatest of the Velocette 500cc singles.*

Below: *The Thruxton had Brooklands-style "cans" (exhausts); the strange Velocette system for pre-loading the rear suspension (the shock absorbers could be moved in an arc); and (above all) immense style.*

Right: *Hyper-development kept singles like the Thruxton alive even as twins such as this 1959 Constellation were beginning to become obsolete. Enfield's Constellation, Interceptor and Meteor twins were very fast.*

1956 BSA Gold Star

There is a select group of motorcycles which are so firmly embedded in the collective psyche that they are always known by their nicknames. The DBD34 Goldie is one of them.

The origin of the name is simple enough. In 1937, an Empire Star piloted by Wal Handley won a race at Brooklands at an average speed of over 100 mph, thereby earning him a gold star. Birmingham Small Arms promptly seized on the name and applied it to a clubman's racer, a machine that was to remain in production from 1937 to 1962. In late roadster trim, the Goldie delivered 37.5 bhp, and the clubman racer was good for maybe 5 bhp more – though many people simply hotted up their roadsters to Goldie specs, or made their Goldies street-legal.

The engine is the raison d' etre of the Goldie; the frame is nothing remarkable, being based on regular "cooking" BSA singles. In roadster trim, with an Amal Concentric carburettor instead of

the GP carb of the Clubman, the engine will just about run below 2000 rpm; furthermore, with the racing carburettor fitted, it's rough below 3000 and won't run at all below 2000.

As so often with classic bikes, light weight (about 350 lb/160 Kg dry) and small frontal area explains the phenomenal performance of a motorcycle with an engine delivering only about

40 bhp; but light weight was also useful in view of the frankly inadequate brakes and the less-than-perfect suspension. Unimpeded induction and exhaust help, too.

By modern standards, the 'bars sport a veritable forest of levers, but they were all essential. The starting drill was to retard the ignition fully, set up the engine on the compression stroke with the help of the decompressor, then KICK for all you were worth. Once it was running, both the rev counter and the speedo read "backwards" (anticlockwise).

Many riders fantasize about a "new Goldie," a fractionally detuned, street-legal race replica. Well, it's been done by Ducati and others. But modern racing bikes are so much more complex and powerful than the Goldie that such machinery is not only impractical; it would be literally impossible to maintain it in race trim for anything like everyday use.

83

Left: *The Norton Commando 750 – this is a 1969 LR or "Long Range" model – was a better bike than its short-lived successor the 850 (actually 828cc) because the engine was smaller and vibrated less. Incredibly, the Isolastic rubber engine mounting did not wreck the handling.*

Below: *Triumph's Trident was essentially a Speed Twin sawed in half and with a third cylinder stuck in the middle. It achieved some racing success after its introduction in the early 1970s, but it was only the Triumph's superior handling that enabled it to hold off the Japanese for as long as it did.*

today than they were in the 1950s or even the 1960s, and they just couldn't afford them then. A look at anyone's home will tell the story. Carpets have replaced linoleum; colour televisions have replaced black and white; stereos have replaced record players. We drink bottled water, something that was formerly regarded as an eccentricity of the rich. We live in an era when Honda can make a truly ugly single, with every line of the design wrong, and call it a homage to the British single, and we buy it because we can't get the real thing.

But in truth, this is often the fate of the greatest classics: they bloom and then they die. The money is in the ordinary motorcycles, the ones that the masses buy, the reliable, boring, but *effective* motorcycles which (if the manufacturer wishes) can also support an altogether smaller number of flagships and classics – which are by no means always the same thing.

There is another problem with classics. For the most part, they exemplify the French proverb: *ils ont les fautes de leurs qualités*, they have the faults of their qualities. Perfect road manners on the winding back roads are paid for on long highway journeys, when you have time to think about hard seats, unyielding suspension, and

buzzy engines. Raw acceleration is paid for in decreased reliability and heavier clutches. Slim, elegant designs are executed at the expense of ease of access to the engine components. Smoothness costs top-end power. A low purchase price often buys you a motorcycle that will rapidly lose its looks, and which it may be cheaper to replace than to repair a few years down the road; uncompromising quality can bring with it a price tag that no-one can afford, and speedy bankruptcy for the manufacturer.

In real life, things are not even this simple. There are national characteristics to be considered, too. Italians will put up with a lot in the way of dubious electrics and poor finish, in return for something that looks good overall and is *fast*. Enough Americans will put up with a self-propelled cement mixer, just because it is American, for Harley-Davidson to stay in business. But most people want a machine that is fast and reliable, well-made and affordable, sweet-handling on the back roads and adequate on the highway. They are unwilling to make the sacrifices that are needed to get a true classic: less flexibility for more power, less speed for more comfort and reliability, less comfort for tighter handling.

Before we look at the Japanese, who so clearly came to dominate the world motorcycle industry during the 1960s, it is worth taking a quick look at which significant European manufacturers survived, and how.

In England, for so long the world's leading motorcycling nation, there were three big manufacturers: Norton, Triumph and BSA. Norton bikes were the best built and the best handling, but their handling (and the "Isolastic" engine mounting, which removed the worst of the vibration) kept the big twin alive beyond its natural life-span much as the Featherbed frame had kept the single on an artificial life-support system. Triumphs were quickest, though when it came to the corners the Norton had it all, hence the fashion for Tritons: Triumph motors in Norton frames. And BSAs were a good compromise, but definitely third place; when they dropped

Below: The BSA Rocket 3 was pretty much a "badge engineered" Triumph Trident, albeit with the cylinders slanted slightly forward to make it look a little different. The Mk II, shown here, was somewhat less ugly than the original but it was now severely outdated: a drum front brake on a "superbike" was just not on. Rocket 3s are even rarer today than Tridents.

DEATH and REBIRTH

the Gold Star in 1962, many people felt that they had lost the right to exist.

Triumph and BSA were now under one roof, and they did make an effort to bring out something really new: a triple, which was sold as the Triumph Trident and the BSA Rocket 3. This was (and is) a motorcycle which generates strong feelings. Its advocates say that it was the first of the affordable "superbikes," the 100 mph-plus machines that would dominate the next decade; they point out, not unreasonably, that Broughs, Vincents and MV Agustas had never been even in sight of the average rider's budget, and that while there had been other popular machines where 100 mph was no problem (such as the Goldie), most of them were fairly one-dimensional. Its detractors say that the triple was cobbled together on an inadequate budget from an unlikely assortment of parts, which it was; it was effectively a Speed Twin that was sawn in half and then "opened up" to accept a third cylinder. Many people also thought it was ugly, but it *was* quick.

Velocette was on the way out, but they were still building what many regard as the best singles ever, while Royal Enfield was still introducing whole new models, such as the 26 bhp Continental GT "Café Racer" of 1965, which offered much the same nominal bhp from 248cc as had the 1000cc Brough Superior SS80 forty years earlier (albeit with vastly more torque). A "baby Goldie," the Continental weighed 300 lb and was good for 80 mph or more, just like the SS80. This particular Enfield died in 1967, though the 736cc Interceptor twin continued until the early 1970s.

Above: *To some extent, Ducati thought like Norton. Instead of radical redesigns, they relied on superb cycle parts and hopped up traditional singles with ingenious tricks like desmodromic valve operation.*

Right: *Some people love Ducati singles like this 450 Mk 3, but they are demanding mistresses: hard to set up properly, beset with Italian electrics, and possessing a beauty which has to be in the eye of the beholder.*

Below: *From 1925 to 1967, though not continuously, BMW made "half twins," shaft-drive vertical singles with clear design debts. This is a late 250cc model, probably an R27.*

Right: *All that Sanglas ever built, from 1949 to their demise in the 1980s, was ohv singles; their oversquare (89.5 x 79mm) 496 cc engine was well made and delivered a reliable 27 bhp, but a* relatively high price and somewhat unexciting performance means that few of these solid motorcycles are seen in private hands; most went to the Spanish police during the Franco regime.

DEATH and REBIRTH

1972 Yamaha 195cc

YAMAHA, A LONG-ESTABLISHED manufacturer of pianos and musical instruments, entered the motorcycle market in 1954; their badge to this day is a triple tuning fork motif. Like their rivals, Honda, they made their name with lightweight motorcycles fitted with jewel-like motors which ran at unheard-of speeds and delivered extraordinary performance for their size. This 1972 Yamaha RD200 delivered 22 bhp from a tiny 195cc twin; only 5 bhp less than a Triumph T5 Speed Twin, though it is hard not to suspect that the Triumph's horses were bigger. "Real" motorcyclists still scorned such motorcycles as "toys," but more and more people were attracted into motorcycling by these unintimidating, affordable machines.

A rev limit of 8,500 rpm on an affordable roadgoing motorcycle was all but unbelievable in 1972; as, for that matter, was an electric start on a motorcycle of less than 200cc.

As long as engine sizes remained small, handling was not too much of a problem; but the early 1970s were when bigger Japanese motorcycles were deservedly called "flexi-flyers."

Although Honda was a staunch believer in four-strokes, the two-stroke engine was the key to the success of most other Japanese manufacturers. The power stroke on every revolution from every cylinder meant that very high bhp/litre figures were attainable, especially with small engines: even road-going motorcycles regularly offered over 100 bhp/litre, which was just about the maximum that was ever extracted from (for example) a Manx Norton.

Not only were the engines very powerful for their size: they were also clean, neat, reliable and easy to maintain. Often, though, they were not maintained: they were bought as toys, and treated as toys, then left to gather dust in suburban garages and mini-storage units.

In Italy, recovery from World War Two was just about accomplished, and the Italians were resuming their interrupted industrialization. Being Italians, they wanted more speed than they could afford; a young man would rather have a fast motorcycle than an ordinary motor-car. Also, Italy's climate was undoubtedly kinder to motorcyclists than England's. It needed to be: deliquescent electrics, and steelwork with all the rust resistance of a battered tin can, made Italian motorcycles very trying indeed to ride in anything other than dry weather. It was not true that you could park your Ducati outside the pub in drizzling rain, only to find when you came out that it was a heap of rust surrounding a light-alloy engine, but it seemed like it.

Ducati's roadgoing desmodromic singles (they began life as racers during 1956) came out in 1969, as 250cc, 350cc and 450cc semi-racers, and a year later they produced the first of their 90-degree V-twins, albeit with spring-closed valves instead of positively-closed. The desmo twin would appear later, and this would be the machine that would carry them on into the 1990s, but these are machines that belong in the next chapter.

The old-established firm of Moto-Guzzi brought out a new 703cc transverse V-twin, using a motor that had originally been

Below: The Honda CB92 of 1962 was a 124cc four-stroke twin with a 10,500 rpm bloodline. It exhibited superb (if not always very long-lived) finish, but the styling left much to be desired.

Right: The first Honda Benly in 1957 was an ugly 97cc single, but the name was recycled. This 250cc Benly twin was one of the first where they got the styling half-way right.

Left: *As technology increasingly left Harley-Davidson behind, style became everything. The long, skinny forks of a "chopper" made cornering precarious, but with a tiny "peanut" tank the machine was no mile-eater anyway.*

Above: *The Honda CB450 first appeared in 1965; this is a 1970 model. Early CB450s were black – the fabled "Black Bomber" – and ugly but quick. The dohc engine delivered power equivalent to that of most 650s of the period.*

developed for the improbable *Mulo Meccanico*, a short-lived (1960 to 1963) half-track tricycle for the Italian army. In this first form, the V7, the new Guzzi was a "soft" tourer with more than half an eye to BMW buyers and in particular to police markets (where its modest 40 bhp was still further downrated to 35 bhp), but in 1969 it grew to 747cc and gained another 5 bhp, to put it on a par with the 45 bhp Vincent Rapide of an earlier era. Once again, this machine would form the basis of all future Guzzis, well into the 1990s.

Laverda paid Honda the pretty compliment of looking long and hard at the 305cc CB77, then bringing out a 600cc version of the same machine with classic Italian looks and handling; they went for the upper end of the market, with a well-made, quick, reliable, overhead-cam twin. Otherwise, Italian makers were carrying on with what they had always done: making stylish tiddlers, along with high-tech racers which carried the flag but were not anything like the tiresome little road bikes which paid for the racing programmes.

In Germany, BMW continued to plough their own furrow with expensive, beautifully made, extremely reliable machines which were, however, rather heavy and rather underpowered; and by the

DEATH and REBIRTH

end of the 1960s, despite police sales, fewer than 5000 motorcycles a year were leaving the factory gates. On rarity alone, never mind quality, these were classics.

Then, in 1969, the new BMW "stroke" series (so-called because the first models were all suffixed "/5") appeared. The engines were much stronger and more modern than their predecessors (though they were, of course, still flat twins), the frames were more rigid, there was more "feel" everywhere, and there were such mod. cons. as an electric starter. The nomenclature was also simplified: the R50/5 was a 32 bhp 500 (actually 494cc), the R60/5 was a 40 bhp 600 (599cc) and the R75/5 was a 50 bhp 750 (745cc). Note that 50 bhp: the new BMW was sluggish by modern standards, and was hard put to exceed 110 mph (the published top speed was 175 kph, 108.5 mph), but this was 5 bhp more than a Vincent Rapide.

In the United States, of course, Harley-Davidson continued to make huge, agricultural V-twins. The new "shovelhead" engine replaced the old "panhead" in 1966, in both 74 cid and 80 cid (1340cc) versions, but 60 bhp was the most that they extracted from these monsters; the regular FL version delivered 54 bhp, about the same as a Triumph 750 twin, but the Harley weighed anything up to 200 pounds more …. Elsewhere in the world, various archaic bikes were kept alive by protected markets. Examples included the Spanish Sanglas single, mandatory for Franco's police; the Indian Enfield, so durable that it was frequently passed on from father to son; and the mostly geriatric and unreliable motorcycles of the Communist bloc.

Small wonder that the mass market, for all but the most utilitarian of mopeds (which were still made in many European countries), passed to Japan. Most specifically, it passed to Honda, because Kawasaki was still mired in such dire knock-offs as the W1 copy of the BSA 650cc twin (their first motorcycle was the B8, a 125cc two-stroke from 1962), while Yamaha's scooters and mopeds were nothing like as good as their pianos and guitars.

Honda, though, had already enjoyed considerable success with the 305cc CB77 Super Sports Twin when they introduced the CB450 in 1965. Soon christened the Black Bomber, it offered the power of a 650cc British twin with the smoothness of a much smaller machine. It was spectacularly ugly, with its "backwards" fuel tank and its misused chrome, but it went very quickly. The only thing that stopped it sweeping the board was that no-one could believe that a dinky little overhead-cam twin with an unheard-of rev limit could possibly be reliable. Among a bewildering variety of other models, with an incredible range of capacities from the 50cc "scooterettes" and the S65 miniature sports bike upwards, Honda made more and more inroads into everyone else's markets.

The thing about Honda was that, like the manufacturers of old, it was founded by an individual with vision; and although it is fashionable to mouth the conventional platitudes about how Soichiro

Left: *This elegantly-faired 1965 Triumph T120R was a racer, but retained the Triumph hallmark luggage rack on the tank. It well illustrates the close relationship between road bikes and club racing, which survives to some extent to this day. The increasing specialization of racers does, however, mean that lessons learned on the GP track are ever less relevant to everyday transport.*

Above right: *The Matchless G80CS push-rod single was introduced in 1961: this is a 1967 model, two years before production ended. It was a "do-anything" machine that was very successful in trials (off road/dual sport) riding, as well as being eminently suitable for everyday transport. Note the trials-inspired high-level (and heat-shielded) exhaust.*

Right: *In the 1950s, Moto-Guzzi's horizontal singles were very long in the tooth, and although they were still as inventive as ever in the racing department, their two-strokes for everyday transport were sometimes odd. In the era of the Lambretta and the Vespa, this 200cc "Galletto" of 1958 could, however, offer the weather protection (and spare wheel!) of a scooter and the stability of a motorcycle.*

Honda was part of a team, and about Japanese management by consensus and so forth, the truth is that as long as the founder was in the driving seat (or rather, in the saddle), Honda quite simply led the world. Soichiro died as this book was being written; the news brought tears to my eyes, not least because he was the last of the great enthusiasts to head a major motorcycle-building empire.

It is true that in those early days no Japanese motorcycle could hold a candle to British or Italian motorcycles when it came to handling: throughout the 1960s and 1970s, the "hinge in the middle" handling of Japanese motorcycles (together with the complete lack of grip of early Bridgestone tyres) was not an insult, but the unvarnished truth. On the other hand, Hondas were comfortable, reliable, oil-tight, and fast (provided you did not want to go around corners). They were also very, very good value.

The net result was intriguing. While Hondas were selling to people who had never owned a motorcycle before, "real" motorcyclists the world over refused to take them seriously. In Europe, they were disregarded because they did not handle very well, and in the United States they were disregarded because they were not big enough or fast enough. Little did they know that in due course both problems would be solved. In fact, it was one Honda that changed the face of motorcycling, the 750cc transverse four of 1969.

DEATH and REBIRTH

Above: *Lifestyle was what Harleys were about; the "outlaw" lifestyle, though many respectable citizens bought Harleys in order to appear more interesting than they were. Ignore the bike: look at the "styling cues" on the rider, the fingerless gloves, tattoos, chained wallet, cowboy boots, beard and beer-belly.*

Left: *This neat 1964 Lambretta 200 is the very opposite of the big, greasy, powerful motorcycle. In the 1960s, blue-jeaned "rockers" on motorcycles used to pick fights with immaculately dressed scooter-riding "mods," whose habit of wearing parkas emblazoned with the Union Jack led to the rocker slogan "Fly the flag – hang a Mod!"*

Above and below: *In the 1970s, Triumph technology lagged more and more. For motorcycles over 500cc the parallel twin was obsolete, and the triple was* *always a hybrid which owed too much to parallel-twin thinking, unlike (for example) the Laverda triples. Even the styling was suspect; the T160 Thunderbird III* *below has awful "ray-gun" silencers and an averagely-ugly paint job. But they were fun to ride, and even to race, as Rob North shows in the picture above.*

5

The
SUPERBIKE
ERA

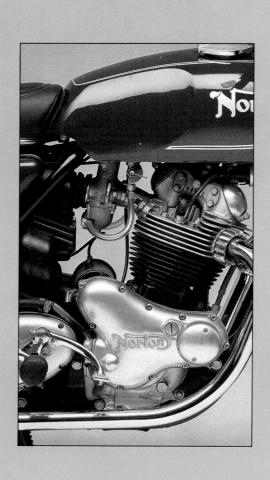

Above: *Norton's Mk 3 850
Commando.* Main picture: *1976
BMW R90S.*

THE SUPERBIKE ERA

"THERE IS A TIDE in the affairs of men, which, taken at the flood, leads on to fortune ...." Shakespeare wrote these words in *Julius Caesar*, but as the 1960s slipped into the 1970s there was a strange new tide in motorcycle-building: the market for ultra-powerful motorcycles was suddenly revealed as enormous.

The reasons are probably twofold. On the one hand, people had more money than ever before and could afford to buy more toys, and even the most dedicated lover of high-powered motorcycles has to admit that by the time you are looking at 120 mph superbikes, you could probably run a modest car for much the same money; a superbike is something you buy because you want it, not because you need it.

Also, Honda (and to a lesser extent the other major Japanese manufacturers) had created an enormous "nursery" or "farm" market, consisting of riders who had learned to ride on small motorcycles, and who now wanted to graduate to something bigger and more powerful.

Which of these two arguments is more important is disputable, and it probably doesn't matter very much anyway, but there can be no doubt that after about 1969, the *minimum* top speed that a motorcycle needed in order to be taken seriously was 100 mph.

At the end of the last chapter, I said that the Honda 750 transverse four was the bike that changed the face of motorcycling. In fact, the big Honda was only part of a tide that also included the new "stroke" series BMWs and which would, in a matter of months, also embrace the Ducati 90-degree twin, and which would soon include many other dramatic machines. For that matter, the whole movement had been prefigured by Ducati's porky-looking but very powerful V4 Apollo, which never made it much beyond prototype form in 1964: the strange-looking 1257cc engine, which resembled four singles more than two twins, is said to have delivered 80 bhp with the option of lots more – potentially well over the 100 bhp mark.

There were, however, two very important things which set the Honda apart from all the rest. In the first place, it was not

Above and above left: *After the blindingly-fast, two-stroke "flexi-flyer" triples of the late 1960s, Kawasaki took another route to power and notoriety in the mid-1970s: huge dohc transverse fours. The 1972 Z1/Z900 offered 82 bhp. Shown are two Z 900s, one in stock trim and the other illustrating that nothing succeeds like excess.*

Left: *Ducati's modern V-twins first appeared in 1971 and offered classic styling, superb handling, and a relatively simple engine. This 750SS has desmodromic valve gear, which is a swine to adjust, but on its' day, can top 200 kph (124 mph).*

Right: *BMW's uncharacteristically-vivid 67 bhp R90S (1973-1976) could exceed 200 kph/124 mph and was an extraordinary combination of relatively docile tourer and thundering superbike. Lightening the flywheel and reworking the heads made it really quick.*

1972 Triumph T150 *T*RIDENT

T HE TRIDENT WAS TRIUMPH'S first "superbike," before the term was invented; indeed, the word may first have been used of the three-cylindered Trumpet. The Bonneville ancestry could hardly be clearer: in profile, it is impossible to see that the bike is not a conventional parallel twin. But the extra cylinder allowed a reduction in individual piston masses, higher reciprocating speed, and fifty per cent more power impulses in a given number of revolutions. The improvement was not as much as one might have hoped, though: about 53-54 bhp, only ten per cent more than a good Bonnie, and the machine weighed 468 lb.

The original T150 (very much like the machine shown here) was announced in 1969 for the 1970 model year; it was followed by the T150V from 1972 to 1975, and then the 503-lb T160 until 1977.

The new 3-cylinder engine was not really competitive with contemporary Japanese or Italian machinery, but it had the advantage of being installed in a

frame which could just about hold its own against a Japanese four even when powered by the old Bonneville parallel twin. The notorious overheating problems,

and the relative lack of power, are partially explained by Triumph's difficulty in keeping all three bores in line ….

A rider's-eye view of the Trident reveals a typical 1970s British cocktail: Lucas electrics, Smiths' instruments, and a putrid paint colour.

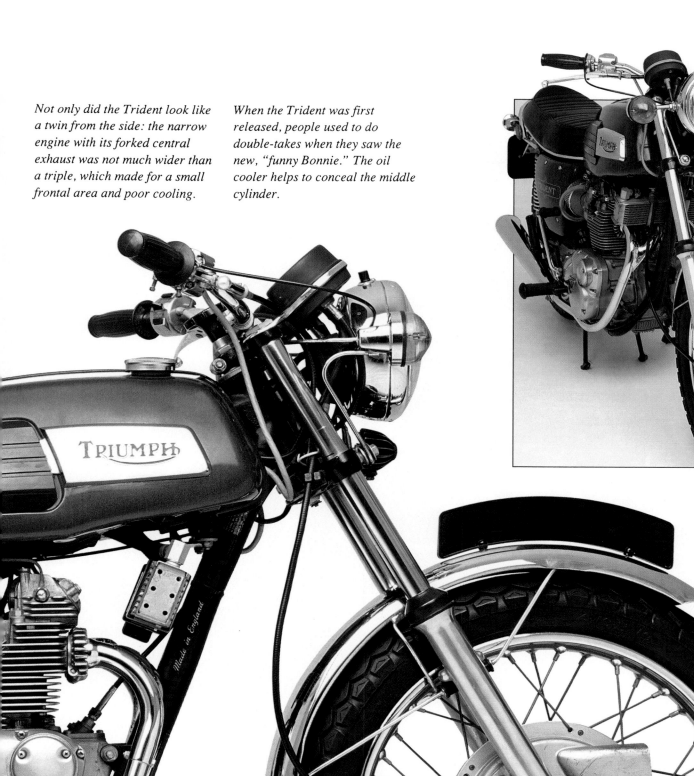

Not only did the Trident look like a twin from the side: the narrow engine with its forked central exhaust was not much wider than a triple, which made for a small frontal area and poor cooling.

When the Trident was first released, people used to do double-takes when they saw the new, "funny Bonnie." The oil cooler helps to conceal the middle cylinder.

The Trident was also available as the B.S.A. Rocket Three, which was even less successful. The cylinders of the BSA were tilted forwards; this engine also formed

the basis of the T160V. The most famous Triumph triple was the "Slippery Sam" racer; Les Williams's bike inspired a line of replicas.

Above: *Suzuki's two-stroke triple GT750 "Water Buffalo" was introduced in 1970. It had remarkable performance, but its thirst was prodigious; it must have been about the most dipsomaniac 750 ever built. Nor was the frame of the "Kettle" equal to the power.*

Below: *Even more unconventional than the Water Buffalo was the 27 bhp DKW/Hercules W2000 of the mid-1970s. Although probably the handsomest Wankel-engined bike ever made before the Norton Classic, no-one trusted Wankels. and it did not last long.*

evolutionary. Like most Honda designs it was totally new, and it was revolutionary. In the second place, it was a mass-production motorcycle. It was not the first transverse four, these had been common in racing for years, and had even appeared in very limited production on road-going bikes like the MV Agusta, but no-one had ever entered series production with such an engine.

With an actual capacity of 736cc, it would pull smoothly in top gear from 1000 rpm to the 8,500 rpm bloodline: from under 20 mph to over 120 mph, all in one gear. Blessed with about 67 bhp, it accelerated very quickly indeed, and in the United States it was cheaper than a BSA or Triumph triple. Decried by many because it was "only" a Honda, it was nevertheless an instant classic.

The handling was still porcine, it was true, but at least they had sobered the pig up and taken away its roller-skates. The same could not be said of its immediate contemporary, the Kawasaki Mach III two-stroke triple. The Kwacker offered even more mind-boggling acceleration (along with a staggering noise and a trail of blue smoke from the unbelievably thirsty motor), but this was not merely a drunken pig on roller skates; it was a *blindfold* drunken pig on roller skates, the original "flexi-flyer." If you can find any of the early two-stroke triples that has not been wrapped around a lamp-post, seized solid or left to die of neglect, you have found another classic, albeit one of technical and historical interest rather than one for riding.

The immediate reaction of the British to these machines was twofold. On the one hand, they tried to get ridiculously large amounts of power out of totally unsuitable engines: the 828cc Commando 850 not only vibrated like a jack-hammer, but in its "Combat" competition trim it was also rather fragile. What was

more, such "mod. cons." as were added were strictly afterthoughts: the electric foot never worked properly, and many owners treated it merely as a power-assist to the kick start.

The other British reaction was a much better idea. Firms like Colin Seeley and others started putting Japanese motors into decent frames. They also cottoned on to the useful idea of adding brakes, which were signally underwhelming on *all* early Japanese superbikes. In the dry, they might or might not prove acceptable, but in the wet, the undrilled disks and non-sintered pads might well deliver a delay of anything upwards of half a second before they suddenly bit – hard.

In 1970, as already mentioned, Ducati's 750SS entered the stakes: a lighter, narrower, better-handling, better-braked bike than anything from Japan, but still lacking in the horsepower department (50 bhp at the rear wheel, maybe 60-65 bhp at the crankshaft), and significantly more expensive than the Japanese. The electrics were still suspect, too, and the finish was nothing like as good as it should have been. But it was another superbike.

Then, in 1971, Laverda improbably introduced a new twin-cylinder superbike, the vivid orange 750 SFC. The actual output is disputable, but it almost certainly exceeded 65 bhp at the crankshaft – all that is necessary even for a 120 mph superbike.

In 1972, Kawasaki upped the ante in the four-cylinder stakes with the 900cc Z1. An incredible 82 bhp was now available straight out of the box, and the massive and almost indestructible engine lent itself readily to go-faster modifications: replacement pistons, cams, valves, exhausts and more were soon made available by a wide range of aftermarket suppliers such as Yoshimura, Moriwaki and Vance and Hines, to name but three of the best known. A street-legal 90 bhp was comparatively easy, and 100 bhp was in reach.

At this point, though, several *caveats* need to be entered. The first is that Japanese horses are notoriously smaller than Italian ones, and Italian ones are smaller than German ones, while British and American horsepower figures were traditionally a product of the marketing department.

The second is that Japanese superbikes were overwhelmingly aimed at the American market, where sustained high speeds are all but unknown and the standing quarter mile is everything. In other words, whereas the buyer of a Ducati would expect to ride at speeds in excess of 100 mph, and to explore from time to time the absolute top speed of the machine, the buyer of a Z1 would not. He might touch 100 mph once or twice, way out in the desert, but he would not expect to ride at such speeds, and the hysterical imposition of the blanket 55 mph limit in the United States in 1973 meant that if he did want to ride fast, he would almost certainly end up in jail.

Left: *This Suzuki GS1000S was typical of the litre-class "Universal Japanese Motorcycle" or "UJM," with its transverse four cylinder double overhead cam engine. The GS1000 first came out in 1977 and was one of the first big Japanese bikes where the handling had the slightest chance of taming the power.*

Right: *In order to keep the width of the CBX engine within (barely) acceptable limits, Honda's engineers moved the alternator behind the engine instead of hanging it on the end of the crankshaft. A downrated engine was produced for the German market, where a "voluntary" 100 bhp limit exists.*

Below: *Honda's 24-valve CBX 1000 was introduced in 1977 and delivered 105 bhp from its almost-unbelievable transverse six. Despite its staggering power, it is a very tractable machine.*

You have only to look at the seats, controls and handlebars of European-market machines and American-market machines to see the difference: a European leans forward onto narrow bars, while an American adopts a sit-up-and-beg posture in a broad, cushioned seat with high handlebars. The American position allows low-speed cruising (up to about 60 mph) for hours on end; the European position will tire you out after eight or ten hours, but you will cover a lot more ground in that time than an American will.

The third important factor is that what had already happened in the United States was beginning to happen in Europe. Motor cars were becoming sufficiently cheap that, if it was mere transport you wanted, a second-hand "banger" was a better bet than all but the smallest, lightest and cheapest motorcycles. Fast bikes were therefore becoming toys, status symbols, things that you bought with disposable income.

With all this in mind, the burgeoning numbers of superbikes makes more and more sense. Even BMW got in on the act in 1973, with not one but two superbikes, the R90/6 and the R90S. Both were overbored developments of the /5 series, but the basic 90/6 delivered a modest (!) 60 bhp, while the R90S could boast an impressive 67 bhp and a top speed of 200 kph (124 mph) if you were lucky. While it is true that the R90S had only the same power as the 750cc Honda four of four years earlier, it was a vastly better finished motorcycle. You had to push it very much harder before it threatened to unseat you on the corners, and its "bikini" fairing and overall design philosophy meant that you could cruise all day at three-figure speeds, assuming the law would let you.

Not all the superbikes that were introduced in the 1970s were successes, though as we have seen before this does not mean that they were not classics. Suzuki's liquid-cooled GT750 triple, generally known as the "Water Buffalo," attracted a small band of devotees but repelled many with its looks and its lumpishness, to say nothing of its thirst. The DKW/Hercules Wankel-engined W2000 was not a commercial success, and Norton's rotary had the longest gestation period of any motorcycle ever, about a decade. Suzuki's 500cc RX-5 rotary of 1975, with its obsessively circular styling theme, was another failure.

The 1974 Honda Goldwing was, however, an outstanding success. Bare, but with all fluids, the 'Wing weighed something like 650 pounds, which accounted for the "Leadwing" gibe that it often attracts in Europe; but with a huge, smooth, water-cooled one-litre flat four to move all that metal, it immediately became the definitive long-distance cruiser for the American market. As soon as it appeared, the full-dresser brigade fell on it like a hen on a blackberry, and its weight frequently approached the 1000 pounds mark. It was embellished with fairings, extra lights, coffin-sized luggage (panniers and top box), crash bars (many protecting areas that could never hit the ground anyway), stereos and soft-drink holders and, of course, "highway pegs," which permitted the rider to assume the gynaecological-table riding position so beloved of American riders, at the expense of putting the rider's feet a good half-meter from either the rear brake or the gearbox.

The 'Wing was a completely different kind of superbike from anything to come out of Europe since the demise of the Square Four about a quarter of a century earlier, and yet, there was something about its grossness that meant it could never be a *gentleman's* motorcycle. It was louche, like a yacht that is only sailed twice a year, or a Rolls Royce with gold-plated trim.

Such considerations of good taste failed to deter anyone, and another superbike race started, based on sheer brute size. Kawasaki upped their big four to 1000cc in 1976, to be followed in 1977 by the Suzuki GS1000 four, a bigger development of their previous 750. Then Yamaha topped the lot with the 1100cc XS1100, with more torque than anyone thought possible but with so much mass that it tended to fall over at parking-lot speeds; an undesirable trait which was not improved by the willingness of the front wheel to "drop in" to low-speed turns.

The 1977 Z1R was allegedly a touring version of the Kawasaki monster four, but it was exposed as a poseur's toy by the size of the fuel tank: sure, it would put 100 miles into the hour, but you would empty the tank in that hour if you tried it.

Rather than let the others make the running, Honda struck back at the end of 1977 with the Honda CBX six-cylinder. Incredibly, this still looked like a motorcycle; in fact, it looked very much like three Speed Twin engines in a row in one frame. Equally incredibly, it was a very tractable motorcycle, which was just as well, because any attempt to ride it fast would remind you that Japanese frame development was still well behind the best that Europe could offer.

The CBX was not the first production six, though. The Benelli Sei, an overhead-cam 750cc transverse six, had had that honour some time before; and if you can find one, that is yet another classic. To this day, there have only been a handful of sixes, and it is hard not to ask if this is because six is simply too many cylinders for a motorcycle.

The water-cooled Kawasaki Z1300 of 1978 really pointed this up. It delivered a nominal 120 bhp, but with the aerodynamics of a brick outhouse and about as much subtlety. For over-engineering, complexity, and weight (especially fully equipped for touring), it has remained the yardstick by which all others are judged. True, it is so heavy that you need to be Superman to handle it, and it makes the CBX look positively svelte, but if you want a lot of motorcycle, this must be yet another classic.

Meanwhile, however, there were several other classics which were not so incredibly vast, and indeed several that were not "superbikes" at all.

In Italy, Moto Guzzi expanded their range of transverse V-twins. The first upgrade in 1971 was to 844cc, from the old V7 special of 1969. Given that the 750 could (just) hit the magic 200 kph/124

Left: *Moto-Guzzi's original transverse twin, the V7 of 1967, had 703cc and 40 bhp. Since then, it has been offered in varying sizes and power outputs; this Spada 1000 is effectively a 73 bhp Le Mans engine in a traditional, powerful tourer/roadster frame.*

Above: *Riding a Kawasaki Z1300 quickly requires considerable strength and bravery; but doing stunts on one, as Arto Nyqvist does, requires something for which there is no real name. Think of him as a circus stunt rider who is riding 120 horses at once ....*

Left: *The first Laverda dohc triples appeared in 1972; they delivered 80 bhp at 7200 rpm, but the single-plane crankshaft created a weird exhaust note. Later Lavs have a 120 degree crankshaft, even more power, and a clutch that would still tax a gorilla.*

THE SUPERBIKE ERA

mph mark on a good day with a following wind, the 850 GT and the 850 California were a bit of a disappointment at only 180 kph (112 mph), but the 71 bhp development of the 850cc engine in the Le Mans (often called a "Lemon" in England) meant that 200 kph was easy and 210 kph (130 mph) was not out of sight; even the 750s went up to 54 bhp.

Then, in 1975, the Italians managed to find another 100cc or so to raise the engine to a nominal 1000cc (actually 949cc) and 65 bhp. The big engine first appeared in the V1000 I Convert, which even with its two-speed, automatic gearbox could just about hit 110 mph, a shade over 175 kph.

Some would say that *all* of the big Guzzis are classics, though purists would dispute the claims of the California with its pseudo-Harley styling (not easy when the engine goes the wrong way!), and the V1000 Convert is definitely a love-it-or-loathe-it machine. By and large, it seems that journalists loathe it, but that those owners who were wise enough to disregard the fevered maunderings of the press love it. The faired Spada, intended as competition to the BMW R100RS (see below), is another whose classic status is disputed, but the Le Mans is of course a classic in everyone's book.

The downscaled Guzzi Vs are also the subject of dispute. The V50 (490cc) of 1977 is often disparaged as slow. It is certainly true that a top speed of only a whisker over 100 mph is hard to understand in a small, light bike with the same nominal power output as a Vincent Rapide, but it still ought to qualify as a minor classic. The 346cc V35, introduced in the home market in the same year as the V50 to take advantage of Italian tax breaks, is still delightful at 33.5 bhp, but is slow by modern standards.

Also in Italy in the early 1970s, Laverda introduced a most improbable 1000cc triple with a 180-degree crankshaft and a curious, loping beat. The clutch was incredibly heavy, but the wonderfully adjustable handlebars and the sheer visceral power of the brute made it exhilarating to ride. "Brute" was the word, though: only a masochist would ride it in town, and on winding

Above: *BMW's big R100 boxers were available in bare roadster trim or with the best fairing ever designed for a motorcycle; the R100RS first appeared in 1976. There is no doubt that the R80 engine is, however, much smoother: purists maintain that the 898cc and 980cc boxers are too big.*

Right: *There will always be some people who like simple, straightforward, old-fashioned motorcycles. Harley-Davidson thrives on this market; Enfield India should be able to do the same; and there are always rumours that the Bonnie (this is a 1970 model) will be revived yet again.*

Below: *On its introduction in 1979, the desmodromic-valve Ducati Pantah was the fastest 500cc bike on the road. With the* rider well tucked in, 200 kph (124 mph) was possible: about the same as a 1000cc Vincent a quarter of a century before. And it handled!

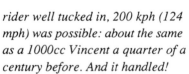

108

roads the tall triple with the weight high up meant that its handling was sometimes more reminiscent of a Japanese machine than of an Italian. In due course, the 120-degree crankshaft smoothed things out a little and delivered even more power, but the "Lav" remained a bike for the True Believer rather than for the everyday rider. The ultimate "Lav" was probably the orange Jota semi-racer, created especially for the British importers. The baby Laverda, the 500cc Alpine twin, is a classic only in the sense that it was rare and well made: you could buy faster bikes for a lot less money from Japanese manufacturers.

Still in Italy, the Ducati twins were now up to 860cc (nominally 900), and the "Hailwood Replica" 900SS commemorated Mike Hailwood's somewhat unexpected Isle of Man T.T. win in 1978. There was also a "baby" Ducati, the 500cc Pantah 90-degree V-twin, which with a little preparation was competitive in Formula 2 racing as well as being a street bike.

One of the greatest bikes of the period, made in much larger numbers, was however both a superbike and a classic. In 1976, BMW introduced the biggest and most powerful production boxer

1975 Norton COMMANDO 850

I N THE DAYS WHEN you could still choose between Nortons, Triumphs and BSAs, it was generally agreed that Nortons were the best-made and the best handling. They were also easily the best looking. The only problem was that there was a constant demand for more power, so Norton kept building bigger engines. The Commando 850 actually boasted 828cc, which was at least 75cc too big and arguably 175cc too big. The "cooking" model did however develop 58 bhp at 5900 rpm, rather more than the Trident triples. The top speed of about 110 mph came up fairly easily, but any attempt to over-rev the engine usually caused it to break; the "Combat" competition engines were particularly fragile.

Any account of late Commandos must alternate between a paean glorifying their advantages and a jeremiad bemoaning their faults. They handled beautifully and they were easy to maintain. A

traditionalist might lament the passing of drum brakes, but the disk stopped the bike better, at least in the dry or when fitted with 1990s brake pad material. The proud boast of "Electric Start"

was, however, for the most part a lie; unless the engine was free and warm, and not always then, the starter was more like a power-assist to the kick-start, but it ran the battery flat anyway. True Brits

felt that the electric foot was a concession to the effete American market, which lacked moral fibre; kick-starting Commandos builds character!

There was really nothing very original about the Commando, but it was put together with such aplomb that it was timeless. With minimal modifications, such as twin disks and an electric starter that worked, it could probably still be sold today.

The pushrod twin was unusually under square at 77mm x 89mm, which accounted in part for its unwillingness to rev much over 6000 rpm: the blood line, beyond which the engine would probably break, was 7000 rpm. Also, it repaid careful running in (or as the Americans so brutally put it, "break-in.") Too much, too soon, and the motor would never reach its full potential.

ever made, the R100RS. Not only did it have a 980cc engine delivering 70 full-sized German horses; it also had one of the most beautiful fairings ever built, wind-tunnel designed for comfortable, fast cruising and for extraordinary resistance to side-winds. In Japanese terms, the top end was unremarkable (200 kph/124 mph claimed, though by "tucking in" behind the fairing the average rider could expect to see 210 kph/130 mph) and the acceleration was modest (0 to 100 kph/62 mph in five seconds), but this was a machine for riding very long distances, very fast indeed. Anywhere that the law permitted (and many places where it did not), the R100RS permitted *average* speeds of over 100 mph (160 kph) for hours on end, with cruising in the 90 to 110 mph range an extraordinarily relaxed experience. If you didn't want the fairing, the "cooking" R100S offered 65 bhp and what amounted to a softer, easier-to-ride R90S. The R100/7, the slug, was a mere 60 bhp and could barely exceed 115 mph.

There were other classics from the 1970s, too. Triumph's "Bonnie" twin stayed in production, and so (just) did the Norton Commando, while the Triumph/BSA triple also survived until 1975. Benelli's Sei (six) was not the only exotic bike in their line-up: they also offered overhead cam fours of 498cc and 231cc. The styling was not pretty, but the engines (especially the smaller one) defied belief.

Small Japanese classics were thinner on the ground, but the lovely little Honda 400/4 must qualify despite its ridiculously heavy clutch. The Suzuki GS750 is widely remembered as the first big Japanese road-going motorcycle with decent handling, and the Kawasaki Z650 was the second; both were transverse fours, the "UJM" or "universal Japanese motorcycle" in the parlance of the time.

The end of the 1970s also saw the introduction of what may be the ultimate "classic/anti-classic," Honda's unbelievably ugly CX500 transverse V-twin. Widely known as the "plastic maggot," and an incredible jumble of engineering innovation and compromise, the CX500 survived (and continues to survive) hideous abuse from its owners. Few people who actually love motorcycling can bear to be seen on one, but in the year 2020 an original CX500 will be a great rarity – simply because no-one takes them seriously. They are run into the ground as commuter bikes or dispatch bikes, then thrown away: somewhere there must be a sort of elephants' graveyard of the things. And this is a good place to stop, and to go on to a chapter which is concerned with spotting classics from about 1980 onwards.

Below: *This Commando Interstate, the property of Paul Thoman, had covered over 100,000 miles when this picture was taken. Admittedly, he looked after it, but any Commando that is properly maintained (not babied!) should be able to do the same, and then go on to do more. Spares are more readily available than for many current production machines.*

Left and below: *The 1975 dohc Honda 400/4 Super Sport extracted no less than 37 bhp from its 408cc; about the same, in fact, as the legendary Goldie 500cc single in roadster trim. And the Honda was a quiet, small, reliable, roadgoing motorcycle whose only drawback was a surprisingly heavy clutch. If you can find an example that has not been neglected, it has to be a classic.*

Below left: *This CX 500 Sports has to be one of the better versions of Honda's transverse V-twin. The original was introduced in 1979 with 45 bhp, later raised to 50, but the CX 650 (actually 670cc) managed 64. Of the 100 bhp Turbo CX650, even Honda admitted that if they could turbocharge that, they could turbocharge anything.*

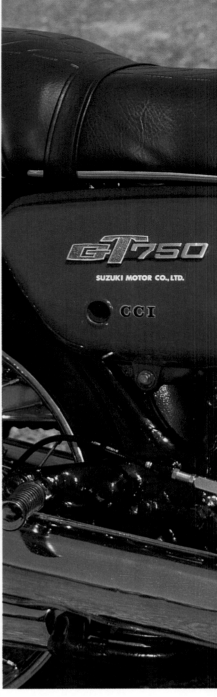

Above: *The exceptionally thirsty two-stroke "Kettle" or "Water Buffalo" was killed by the so-called gas crisis of 1974; it was all too easy to get below 30 mpg (9.4 litres/100 km). But those who still own GT750s love them; the handling is tolerable by 1970s Japanese standards.*

Above: *Six running lights, a headlight, two spotlights, a CB radio, two eagles and a pig (look atop the headlamp "eyebrow"); the owner of this ElectraGlide (in blue, of course) was less worried about aerodynamics and battery drain than about appearance. Even the windshield is engraved, with a Harley and a truck.*

Right: *At its best, a Harley-Davidson custom bike combined the best of the past with a modest degree of modern technology; but to get the classically clean lines and taut handling of a rigid frame, the rider had to sacrifice no small amount of comfort.*

Right: *The X-75 was a short-lived (1973 only) version of the Trident/ Rocket 3. The high bars betray the American specification, despite the English number plate, while the stacked exhausts make a statement all their own. Borrani rims and drum brakes are vintage touches.*

115

Above: *Astonishingly, Ducati V-twins remained competitive well into the 1980s and even 1990s against much more complicated and "advanced" machinery, though as this picture shows, the rider had to "tuck in."*

Left: *After some experiments with R75s and high-level exhausts, BMW introduced the R80GS. Eminently unsuitable though the big boxers might seem, they have done well in such events: this is the 1979 I.S.D.E. (formerly I.S.D.T.)*

Right and top right: *Morini's elegant little 350cc 3.5 V-twins come in three flavours: roadster, sports/racing (right) and off-road (top right). At first, the off-road bike seems improbable; but its' light weight, low centre of gravity and ample power it is in fact a strong contender.*

6

NOW
—and—
FUTURE
CLASSICS

Above: *The 500 cc Enfield Bullet.*
Main picture: *The Triumph
Daytona Sport 1000.*

Now and Future Classics

ITH A VERY FEW exceptions, you need the perspective of a decade or two to be able spot classics, which is why any appreciation of "classics" manufactured since about 1980 is difficult in a book written in the early 1990s.

Let's begin, though, with the clear exceptions. The most glorious must surely be the Hesketh, described by Mick Broome (head of development) as "the last 1950s motorcycle."

It was conceived as a no-compromise gentleman's machine in the Brough Superior tradition. With a 1000cc, four-overhead-cam engine delivering anything from 80 to 90 bhp in standard trim, it was certainly not lacking in the engine department. The brakes, frame and finish were among the finest ever. Its only drawback was that it was heavy (over 500 pounds), though according to press reports, there were also problems with the gear selection. In truth, the problem was that in order to shift smoothly you had to match engine speed to road speed. The average motorcycling journalist, of course, is unaware of such subtleties: their approach is to stamp it into gear and let the clutch and the rear tyre take care of any discrepancies. Ridden sensitively, noiseless changes with or without the clutch were entirely feasible.

Unfortunately, cash-flow problems forced the company out of business within months of the launch in April 1982. A restructured company produced a limited number of bikes to special order, which was still the situation at the time of writing. Anyone who buys a Hesketh should find that spares are no problem. Easton Neston will be as helpful as possible, and the machine is so over-engineered that there is virtually no likelihood of its wearing out, and they will also have a machine which will one day be legendary. The unfaired V1000 and V1000 lightweight (under 500 pounds!) are the ones to go for: the Vampire has an attractive enough fairing, and is much rarer, but lacks the vintage charm of the unfaired bike.

The frame is not chromed; it is nickelled, because chrome would embrittle the Reynolds tubing of which it is fabricated. The paintwork is deep and lustrous, adorned with the Hesketh emblem irreverently known as the "Flying Chicken." The huge, handsome engine with two cams per cylinder is surely the lineal descendant of J.A.P. and Anzani specials for Brough Superior, or the immortal Vincent Black Shadow, but with lots more power. What is not made at Easton Neston is bought in from the best: Brembo brakes, Marzocchi forks. If you can afford it, put your name on the waiting list for a new one.

1990 Enfield India BULLET

THE ENFIELD BULLET 500 is not a replica or a revival; it is a genuine, original Royal Enfield Bullet with all the traditional virtues of the brand – superb reliability, unshakable handling, enormous load-carrying capacity, and much, much more – with the benefit of four decades of improvements in metallurgy, electrics, and general detailing. They just never stopped making them at Thiruvottiyur, just north of Madras in India. Inherently a far more advanced design than any Harley-Davidson, albeit with half the power of even the smallest Milwaulkee machine, the Bullet is perfect whether you want the classic look, or the actual classic virtues: a bike that will run on anything with a higher octane rating than cough syrup, and which the average owner can maintain himself with absolute confidence using reasonably-priced spares.

For years, The Enfield India was kept alive by an artificial life-support system consisting of Indian government orders and protectionist legislation. When at last things were freed up, they had

an "instant classic" on their hands: a reasonably priced, handsome-looking, totally traditional motorcycle. They sold worldwide; they even exported to Japan.

The old 350 Bullet – the traditional mainstay – was supplemented in 1990 by the 500, which could only boast 22 bhp because of its low compression ratio (Indian petrol tankers should

bear a warning saying "Danger – Fairly Flammable") but which was staggeringly flexible. Instrumention (right) is basic in the extreme, but how much more do you really need?

No matter what angle you choose, everything about the Bullet is right: the big drum brakes, the non-unit gearbox with neutral selector, the big, chromed exhaust, the external oil-lines, the wire-laced wheels, the "casquette" headlamp ….

The Bullet is not the motorcycle to buy if you want power: the 350 delivers 17 bhp, the 500 only 22 bhp. But for durability, rideability and sheer style, The Enfield has very few rivals.

Now and Future Classics

At the very other end of the scale, the Indian Enfield 350cc Bullet remained in production at the time of writing, and the 500cc Bullet had been reintroduced in 1990; actually, this was the first time that the bigger Bullet had been made in India. With a very modest price, and much improved quality control and metallurgy over its predecessors, the Enfield is an "instant classic." The 500cc is incredibly torquey and "soft," not least because of the very low compression ratio. The *bomp-bomp-bomp* of the big single is pure nostalgia, and although the performance is distinctly leisurely, the machine will slog along all day at 60 to 70 mph (100 to 110 kph). I would far rather have a new Indian Enfield than an old and probably abused British original, and spares are readily available at distinctly vintage prices!

In the early 1990s, Indian Enfield were also working on overhead cam designs, initially for smaller versions of the basic Bullet but possibly for all models up to and including the 500. The managing director was not indifferent to the idea of an overhead cam four-valve 500cc sports model ….

While you are considering retrobikes, you might also take a look at the MZ 250cc two-stroke singles, especially the 5-speed TS250/

Above: *The Dneipr or Ural 650cc flat twins are roughly World War Two-vintage BMWs with a Russian spin. They are available with and without sidecars (and with and without sidecar drive), but once you have overcome teething troubles you will have a reliable (if slow) motorcycle which is all but unstoppable.*

Left: *All four wheels – front, rear, sidecar and spare – are interchangeable, just like the Wehrmacht originals from which the big Russian twins are copied, and in the event of a spill, anything that is damaged can be kicked or hammered straight again.*

Left: *The only exclusivity about new BMWs is brought about by the price – but keep any BMW for a decade or two, and you will find that you own a bike which attracts attention. "Bricks" like the K100RS shown here are more complex than Boxer twins, but neither is difficult to keep running just about forever.*

Right: *When you ride a BMW, you learn that very few BMW owners are snobs. Most are very experienced riders who have gravitated to BMWs as the perfect combination of power, handling, reliability, simplicity and even price: a bike like this R100GS is economical if you consider how long it lasts.*

1989 BMW K100 RS

THE 1984 BMW "BRICK" – a dohc liquid-cooled in-line four mounted longitudinally and laid on its side – was the first new big BMW since 1923, when the transverse "Boxer" format was adopted. Inevitably the traditionalists screamed, and BMW was both surprised and embarrassed that their customers would not allow them to drop the 980cc Boxer flagships, even though the R100RS had dropped from 70 bhp to 60 bhp (as a result of emission controls) while the K100RS offered a good 90 bhp and 140+ mph as a matter of course. Early machines had their teething problems, such as an embarrassing cloud of smoke on starting and a petrol tank which got very warm indeed, but these were only details and eventually production settled down with the 1000cc fours and their 750cc triple derivatives running alongside the venerable Boxers. One day, the early K-series BMWs will be collectable too ....

BMW's "RS" designation is supposed to come from Rennsport (racing), but what it effectively means is "sports-tourer": sporting enough to go very quickly indeed, but tractable and comfortable enough to ride for very long distances. It is a category that no other manufacturer has ever managed quite so well; both the K100RS "brick" and the R100RS "boxer" are perfectly suited to long-distance European touring.

ABS – anti-lock braking – was a BMW "first" in production bikes, and an enormous contribution to safety. Paradoxically, skilled riders benefited most, as they now knew how much further they could push their luck on poor surfaces.

The K100RS fairing looked much smaller than that of the R100RS, and was probably tougher; but it afforded remarkable protection from wind and rain, even at very high speeds, though pillion passengers sometimes complained of a feeling of suffocation at much over 120 mph. The hand protectors/signals were designed to snap off (and snap back on again) in case of a spill.

Above: *When it comes to collect-ables, sports bikes are normally more desirable than tourers. Exceptions might include "full dresser" Harleys and machines like this 1982 BMW R80RT.*

Below: *As a rule, the rarer and more exotic the bike, the faster it becomes a classic; this 1986 Ducati F1 750 is an "instant classic" while lesser Dukes might take ten or twenty years.*

Right and far right: *The Moto-Guzzi Le Mans 1000 has always been a highly desirable motorcycle, but this '91 will probably not be accorded true "classic" status for a couple of*

decades. Early examples – the 850cc "Lemon" came out in 1974 – are worth more than later models, though the first 1000cc Le Mans (early 1980s) would be more desirable as a "landmark" model.

1 Supa 5. The styling is strange, and it is virtually impossible to get them to tick over smoothly, but they are very forgiving, sweet-handling little machines which will really annoy owners of small Japanese motorcycles when you come to corners, provided only that you have replaced the horrible original Pneumant tyres with almost anything else made in Europe or Japan.

Likewise, the Russian Ural, Dneipr and Cossack derivatives of the BMW are quite fun, especially the sidecar-drive versions. You may however have to replace various bearings, valves and so forth before the machines are anything like reliable.

Yet another retrobike was the Brooklands Motorcycles' "Manx Norton," made in England in the early 1980s with first Weslake, and then (after 1984) Rotax 500cc singles. Simple, fast and beautifully made, these should be classics in their own right.

Going back to more modern machines, the 1000cc four-on-its-side BMW "brick" probably deserves classic status, especially if you buy one of the early ones which smokes ferociously for about a minute-and-a-half when you start it. The smoke is harmless, and it shows that even BMW make mistakes sometimes! Seriously, the 90 bhp "brick" is fast, smooth and comfortable (though the petrol tank gets uncomfortably hot on long journeys), and the "three-quarter brick" (the 750cc triple) is fast, smooth, comfortable and much more "flickable" than the full-size machine: many people actually prefer it. The fully-faired K100RS, or the still more carefully wrapped K1 super-sport, or *any* BMW with anti-lock brakes are the most desirable "bricks."

Among the later Boxers, the R80GS and R100GS on road/off-road bikes have to be classics in anyone's book, especially with the monster competition petrol tanks – though the smaller tank is more manageable, especially when full – and anyone who is much under six feet tall may find the seat rather high. The re-introduced R100RS is nothing like as desirable as the original, because it has a miserable 60 bhp instead of 70 bhp, but it is still better than no

R100RS at all. The R100RT (the "Touring" model), and its smaller brother the R80RT, are pretty much compromises for the American market, with "barn door" fairings; the R100RS is the perfect European tourer.

From Italy, you can still find motorcycles which were (and in many cases, still are, because they are still in production) much the same as those of the 1970s and earlier: Guzzi's V-twins of various sorts (including the Le Mans), various Ducatis (including the Hailwood Replica and the beautifully-faired, fuel-injected Paso 750), Laverdas, and so forth. Arguably, though, there are no really new classics. It seems increasingly likely that Italian motorcycles will settle into the Harley Davidson mould of nostalgia bikes; a lot faster and better handling than Harley-Davidsons, it is true, but still with their basic technology frozen in the past.

Now and Future Classics

Then again, maybe there will be new machines from Italy, just as there have been from Britain. After all, during the 1980s Norton successfully put the Rotary into production as the Interpol II, and, when the police declared themselves fully satisfied, Norton even introduced a remarkably expensive civilian version as the Norton Classic. For one of the most advanced bikes on the road it looks curiously old-fashioned, but that could be as much a styling exercise as anything else. Police who have compared the Norton and the BMW are *very* impressed with the Norton.

By the same token, it seemed at the time of writing that the new, liquid-cooled Triumphs really were going to make it into volume production, though the on-again, off-again performance of previous Triumph "revivals" (dating back to the 900cc Diana/ Phoenix of 1982) leads one to avoid excessive optimism when considering this company. By the time you read this, the Triumph question should have been settled; and if it has been settled favorably, then the new

Left: *The 140 mph (226 kph) "clock" on the Norton Classic is not excessive; you may not be able to wrap the needle around the end-stop, but you can get it close enough. The new Norton is "classic" in more than just looks and name.*

Top left and top: *The elegantly-scripted "Norton" on the tank tells of tradition, but the big twin Brembos on the front are bang up to date and can stop the bike better than any drums ever could. And cast alloy wheels are lighter and run truer than any laced wheel.*

Above: "Classic," they called it; and strangely enough, it is. It was well proven as the Interpol II, and the only fault one could find with the civilian version was the stiff price. This 1988 model was the twenty-fifth civilian Classic to be built.

Right: *Proper engine plates, restrained styling, no art-student graphics; the Classic is truly a machine for today's serious motorcyclist. Rather like a Vincent, it is a big, beautiful engine with motorcycle running gear bolted to it.*

This page: *The styling of the new Triumphs was disappointingly generic, though at least the paint job was reasonably restrained. The new engines were, however, anything but boring; a range of triples and fours with capacities up to 1200cc. This is a Trophy 1200 Sports Tourer with a 9500 rpm bloodline and a 180 mph speedometer; how far you wound the needle around the clock was a matter of bravery (or foolishness) rather than a matter of coaxing the ultimate out of the blocky but surprisingly elegant dohc four.*

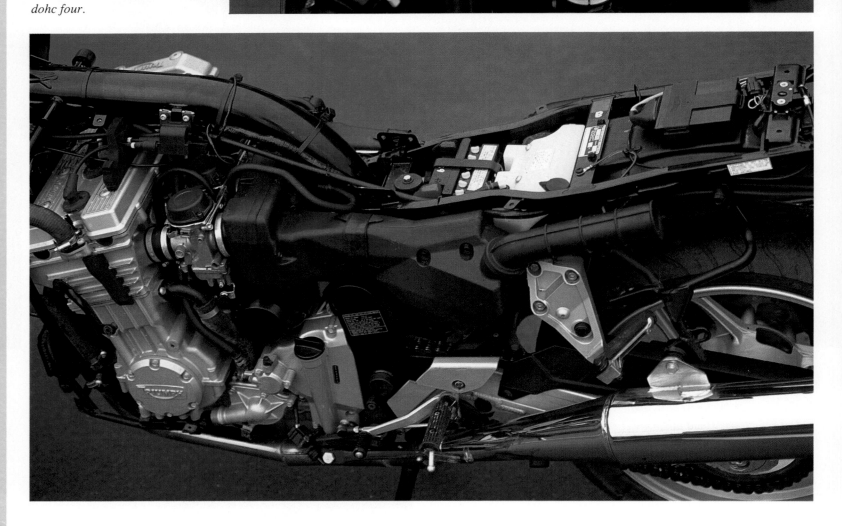

Trumpets will be somewhere between the classicism of the Italians and the endless novelty of the Japanese, which should be rather an attractive combination of features.

Speculations about Triumphs pale, though, beside the question of guessing which (if any) recent Japanese machines might achieve classic status.

At the smallest end of the scale, Honda's lovely little VT250 would be a strong contender. It is one of the smallest V-twins ever made, it was made by a major manufacturer, and it has a superb engine and first-class handling. Little did anyone think in the 1960s that it would ever be possible to praise the handling of a Japanese motorcycle!

At the other extreme, almost any Yamaha V-Max has to be some sort of classic; the only question is what sort. Introduced as a 1200cc V4 with 135 bhp, the output later rose to 145 bhp and outputs as high as 165 bhp have been reported. It is a rather one-dimensional machine, but sooner or later such insane power outputs will be outlawed in more and more countries. If you want the most powerful motorcycle ever built, buy the last V-Max the day before they are banned.

Another big machine that might deserve classic status is the CBR1000, Honda's answer to the Vincent Black Prince, and while we are on the subject of full enclosure, the widely-reviled Honda Pacific Coast will probably prove to be one of those commercial (or at least critical) failures which long after its demise will attract fierce partisans.

In between, the Yamaha LC350 and LC500 quite naturally attract attention as racers-on-the-road, and so does the Suzuki

Left: *Yamaha borrowed styling cues from their awesome, liquid-cooled V-Max V-four street-legal dragster, and applied them to a range of fairly ordinary air-cooled V-twins. The fake air-scoops say "V-Max," but there aren't enough cylinders.*

Below: *Most Europeans entertain mixed feelings about American bikers. They get the best bikes first (except when their weird laws step in), but some of them seem to spend more time posing than actually riding. This is another imitation V-Max at Daytona.*

1990 BMW K1

Every now and then, BMW confound their critics who say that their motorcycles are boring, old-fashioned, low-powered, and fit only for old men – though some of the young men who spout these words might find themselves pushed to keep up with the old men they denigrate. The R90S was one mould-breaker, and the K1 was another. The dohc in-line four was given 16 valves and made to produce exactly 100 bhp, in accordance with the German "voluntary" limit on motorcycle power (which would soon become compulsory if anyone ignored it), but in conjunction with lots of torque and a wind-tunnel-designed fairing, it propelled the motorcycle very quickly indeed. The acid-trip colours met with a mixed reception, however; those who preferred to go very quickly without being noticed were relieved when more sober hues were offered.

Even the instruments are vivid – but there are touches of the older, more conservative BMW in the shape of the switches built into the fairing, and the provision (after the bum-stop has been removed) of a pillion seat and foot-rests. Note, too, the knee-padding on the fairing.

The odd-looking front mudguard is proof that streamlining may sometimes be counter-intuitive; a smaller mudguard would look faster. But then look at the slotting and shaping, and you realize that BMW must have done their homework.

The monolever rear suspension looks weird, but BMW uses it on the R100GS as well as on this K1; and it's very convenient, as well as neat and easy to clean.

Now and Future Classics

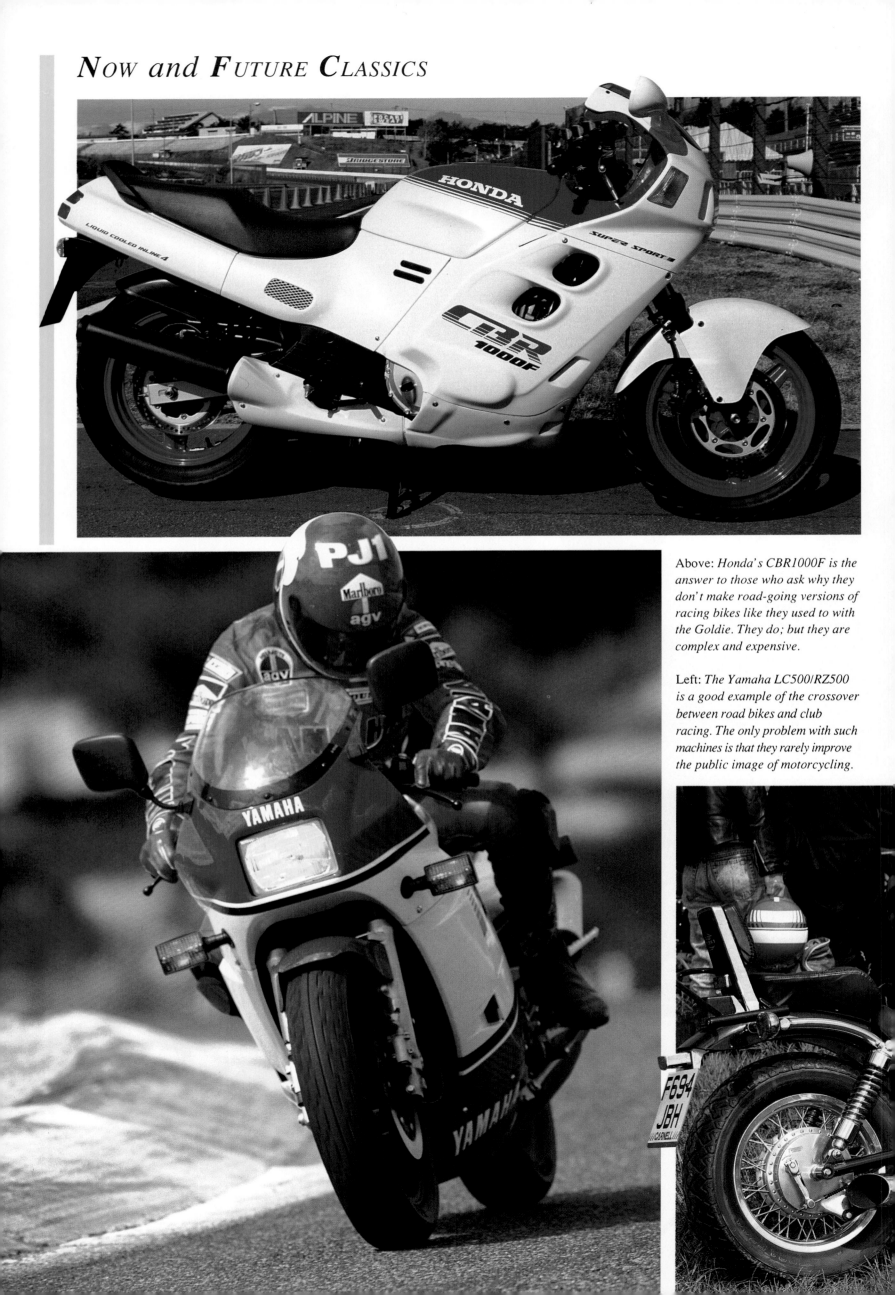

Above: *Honda's CBR1000F is the answer to those who ask why they don't make road-going versions of racing bikes like they used to with the Goldie. They do; but they are complex and expensive.*

Left: *The Yamaha LC500/RZ500 is a good example of the crossover between road bikes and club racing. The only problem with such machines is that they rarely improve the public image of motorcycling.*

Left: *Suzuki's 1400cc Intruder is aimed squarely at the Harley market, like Kawasaki's Vulcan and Yamaha's Virago. Blatant imitations like this are unlikely ever to be classics.*

Above: *Honda's controversial Pacific Coast is very cleverly designed and (mostly) very functional. But imagine it painted in gleaming black with a gold pin stripe, like a Black Prince ….*

RG500 Gamma. The Gamma boasts 95 bhp in a 336-pound motorcycle, but the disk-valve, four-cylinder, two-stroke motor is prodigiously thirsty.

In the altogether quirky range, some of the monster off-road singles like the Yamaha Tenéré might be another candidate for classic status, but I rather suspect that BMW has got that one sewn up with the Paris-Dakar replicas.

The Japanese Harley look-alikes serve for the most part only to drive home the Harley Davidson advertising slogan which said "anything else is less," and the only Harleys worth having have continued to come from Harley-Davidson. The Suzuki Intruder 1400 and the Kawasaki Vulcan 1500 do, however, have a certain over-the-top kitsch appeal. The H-D "softail," with its ingeniously-disguised sprung rear end mimicking a rigid frame, is however the real thing and is probably one of the major classics of a classic line.

These will have to be enough guesses or predictions, because it is impossible to sort out the rival claims of all the amazingly quick road/racing bikes that the Japanese manufacturers flooded the

market with during the late 1980s and early 1990s. They all look wonderful as I write, and no doubt many of them are, but it is only with the perspective of many years that we can rank the classic racers of an era as long ago as the 1930s. Even then, we might argue as to whether the Norton was actually the *undisputed* leader, or whether (say) Velocette or the AJS "Porcupine" should also be given star billing above the title.

Besides, in the long run, what does it matter? As I said in the introduction, no one else would make quite the same selections that I have made for this book, and no-one else would rank the machines in quite the same way. Motorcycles are not just about speed and racing. They are also about touring, going to places we have never seen before or returning to well-loved haunts. They are about gentle rides on back roads, and picnics in meadows. They are about scrambling over rocks and climbing up river beds; they are about sitting around and talking with friends who also ride. They are even about getting to work, but that is not something we should dwell on.

A book about classic motorcycles is a book about dreams, pleasant fantasies which may or may not come true. For example, who has not dreamed of an old lady saying (in return for our carrying her groceries or some such), "Thank you, you have been so kind ... I wonder if you would like the motorcycle that my husband used to ride. A great big thing, it is – a Vincent ...." Or an MV Agusta, or a Brough Superior, or whatever else your dreams run to.

Above: *Honda's NR750 is stunningly styled, but the oval-piston design that Honda racers pursued in the early 1990s must surely be a technological dead-end for road bikes; ultimately, you can get more than enough power from more conventional designs.*

Left: *Like it or not, full enclosure is the wave of the future. Even Italian classics like this fuel-injected, desmo-valved 1991 Ducati Paso 907 are now wearing sheets of plastic and fibreglass for better aerodynamics, easier cleaning, and better protection for both the rider and the engine from the elements.*

Above: *Norton's Commander is the fully-faired version of the rotary-engined Classic. It is a more practical touring machine than the unfaired motorcycle, but the neat and somewhat BMW-like looks of this '90 model lack the charisma of the unfaired machine, which looks more, yes, that's the word – Classic.*

Below: *Never mind "Less is More." This liquid-cooled Suzuki GSX1100G is firmly in the "More is More" tradition of the Big Transverse Four, as established by Honda's 750/4 and the big Kawasaki Z-bikes. It is an excellent motorcycle, but as a "me-too" design it is unlikely ever to become a major-league classic.*

Below: *Perhaps as a reaction to high technology and good handling, people continue to build choppers like this Triumph at Daytona. They rarely see their money back, but most are more interested in making an artistic statement than in commerce.*

Above and right: *Some people call Bimota frame makers, because they use other people's engines; but for that matter, so did Brough Superior. The 1990 Bellaria, above, is one of their more conventional machines, but the Tesi, right, is another matter entirely.*

Facing page bottom: *Shorn of its bodywork, the Tesi is revealed as the "forkless wonder." It first appeared in 1983 with a Honda*

VF400 engine, but this 1990 Ducati-engined version with its "birdcage" frame and hub steering may be the future of fast motorcycles.

A book about classic motorcycles *should not* be an investor's guide, a bean-counter's manual. At most, it might suggest a few machines which, if we buy them now, will save us from saying in ten or twenty or thirty years time, "You know, I could have had one of those, but I didn't think it was worth the money!"

In this book, I hope that I have shared some of my dreams with you; and not merely my dreams, but also the dreams of Albert J. Stevens, George Brough, Val Page, Phil Vincent, Edward Turner, Soichiro Honda, Lord Hesketh and a host of other motorcycle designers and motorcycle lovers, alive or dead. I hope that those who are alive are happy, and that those who are dead are somewhere where you can walk into a huge, oil-and-metal-smelling warehouse, take your pick of any motorcycle ever made, and ride for as long as you want on the back roads and highways of eternity. And I hope that your dreams will come true.

Above: *It is interesting to speculate whether off-road bikes like this Honda XR350R will ever achieve classic status. The answer is "Probably not." Even the Cotton, AJS and other trials classics attract only a very limited number of aficionados.*

Below: *Suzuki's Katanas, first released in a range of sizes in 1980, defined the style of a decade. This GSX 1170 would be fun to own, but it is arguably less of a classic than a stock machine. Buy why do you buy a motorcycle: for fun, or as an investment?*

Facing page top: *You want a classic racer? Well, how about this Ron Haslam-piloted Norton Grand Prix bike from 1991, marking Norton's return to major-league racing with a new motorcycle? It might be excessively interesting as a road bike, though.*

Right: *"Ducati Superbike," it says on the tank; and they were not joking. Just about any Duke ever is a classic, but for a V-twin to remain competitive in 1991 it had to be pretty special. Desmodromic valve gear and fuel injection helped.*

INDEX

Picture Acknowledgements

SIMON CLAY/COLOUR LIBRARY BOOKS: 10 inset, 14-15, 18-19, 24 inset, 28-29, 36-37, 46 inset, 50-51, 54-55, 60-61, 66-67, 78 inset, 82-83, 88-89, 96 inset, 100-101, 110-111, 118 inset, 122-123, 126-127, 134-135
DAVID GOLDMAN: 2-3, 4, 6 above left and right, 7 below, 102 above, 103 above, 137 above, 139 above right, 140-141 above, 141 below
PATRICK GOSLING: 118-119, 125, 129 above, 132, 138-139 above, 138 below, 139 below.
RON KIMBALL: 1

PHIL MASTERS: 128 below, 129 below
DON MORLEY: 8, 9, 10-11, 12, 13, 16, 17, 20, 21, 22, 23, 24-25, 26, 27, 30, 31, 32, 33, 34, 35, 38, 39, 40, 41, 42, 43, 44, 45, 46-47, 48, 49, 52, 53, 56, 57, 58, 59, 62, 63, 64, 65, 68, 69, 70, 71, 72, 73, 74, 75, 76, 77, 78-79, 80, 81, 84, 85, 86, 87, 90, 91, 92, 93, 94, 95, 96-97, 98, 99, 102 below, 103 below and bottom, 104, 105, 106, 107, 108, 109, 112, 113, 114, 115, 116, 117, 120, 121, 124, 128 above, 130, 131, 133, 136 above and left, 136-137 bottom, 140 above left and below left, 142, 143
NATIONAL MOTOR MUSEUM, BEAULIEU: 6 bottom, 7 above, 8 below